This Book Belong To:

Date: _____ Time: _____

Location: _____

Weather Conditions

☀ ☁ 🌤 🌧 🌦 🌨 ⚑ 🌡
☐ ☐ ☐ ☐ ☐ ☐ ____ ____

Firearm:	
Bullet:	Seating Depth:
Powder:	Grains:
Primer:	
Brass:	
Distance:	

Overall Results

☐ Poor   ☐ Fair   ☐ Good   ☐ Excellent

Notes

_____
_____
_____

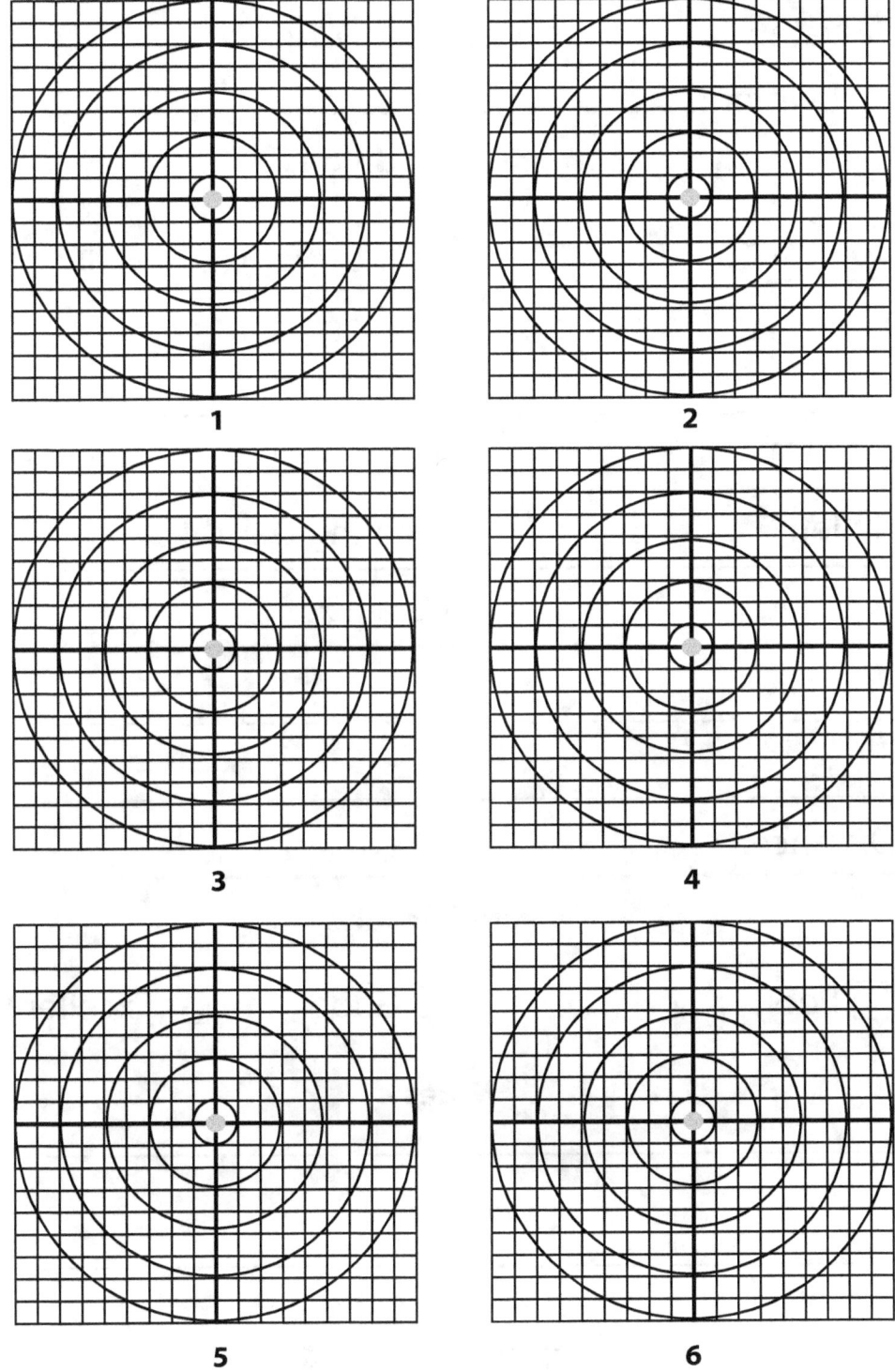

Date: _____ Time: _____

Location: _____

Weather Conditions

☀ ☐   ⛅ ☐   🌥 ☐   🌦 ☐   🌧 ☐   🌨 ☐   🚩 _____   🌡 _____

Firearm:	
Bullet:	Seating Depth:
Powder:	Grains:
Primer:	
Brass:	
Distance:	

Overall Results

☐ Poor   ☐ Fair   ☐ Good   ☐ Excellent

Notes

_____
_____
_____

☆ ☆ ☆ ☆ ☆

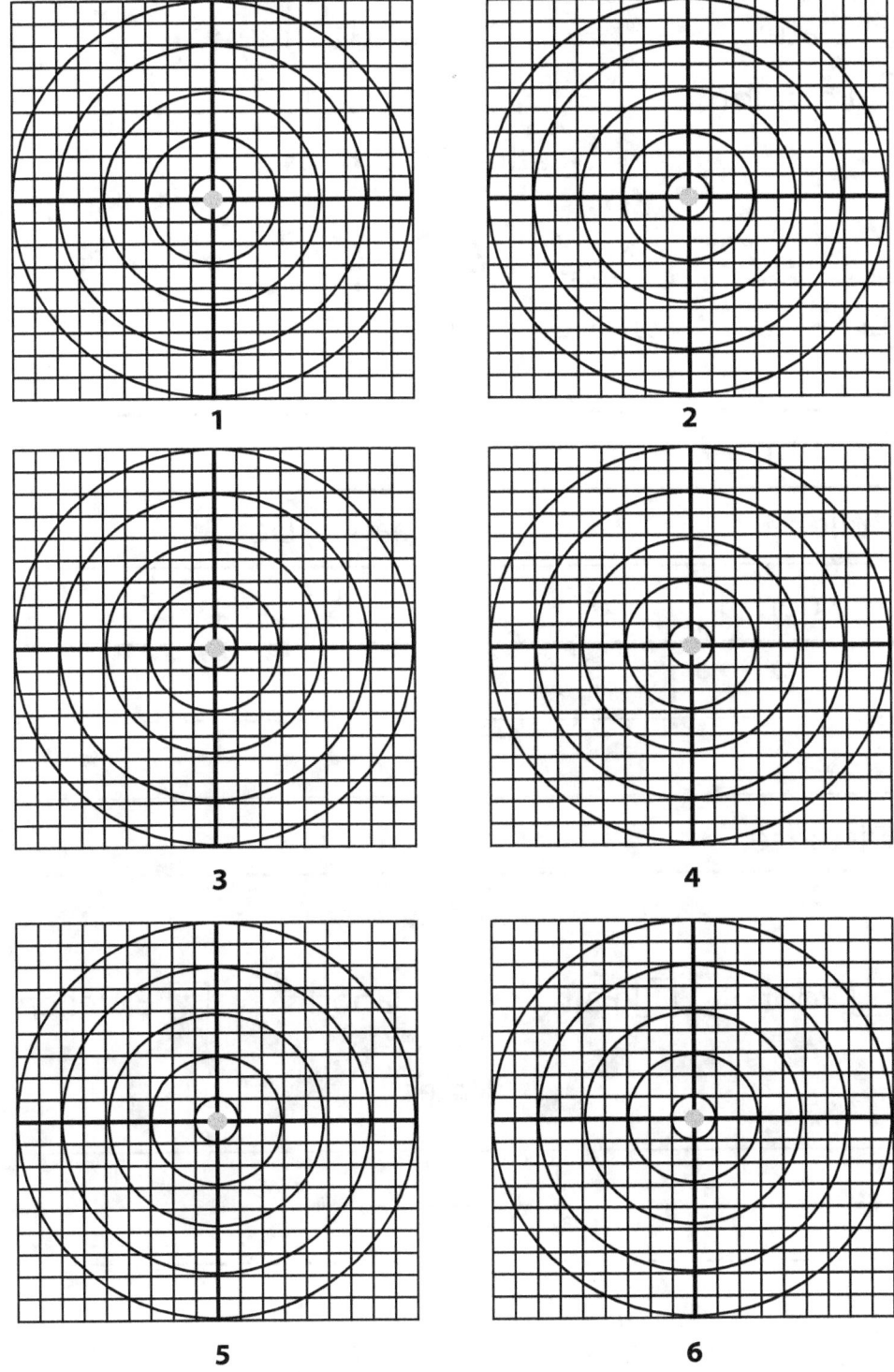

Date: _____   🕐 Time: _____

📍 Location: _____

Weather Conditions

☀️ ☁️ ⛅ ☁️ 🌧️ 🌨️   🚩   🌡️
☐   ☐   ☐   ☐   ☐   ☐   _____   _____

Firearm:	
Bullet:	Seating Depth:
Powder:	Grains:
Primer:	
Brass:	
Distance:	

Overall Results

☐ Poor   ☐ Fair   ☐ Good   ☐ Excellent

Notes

_____

_____

_____

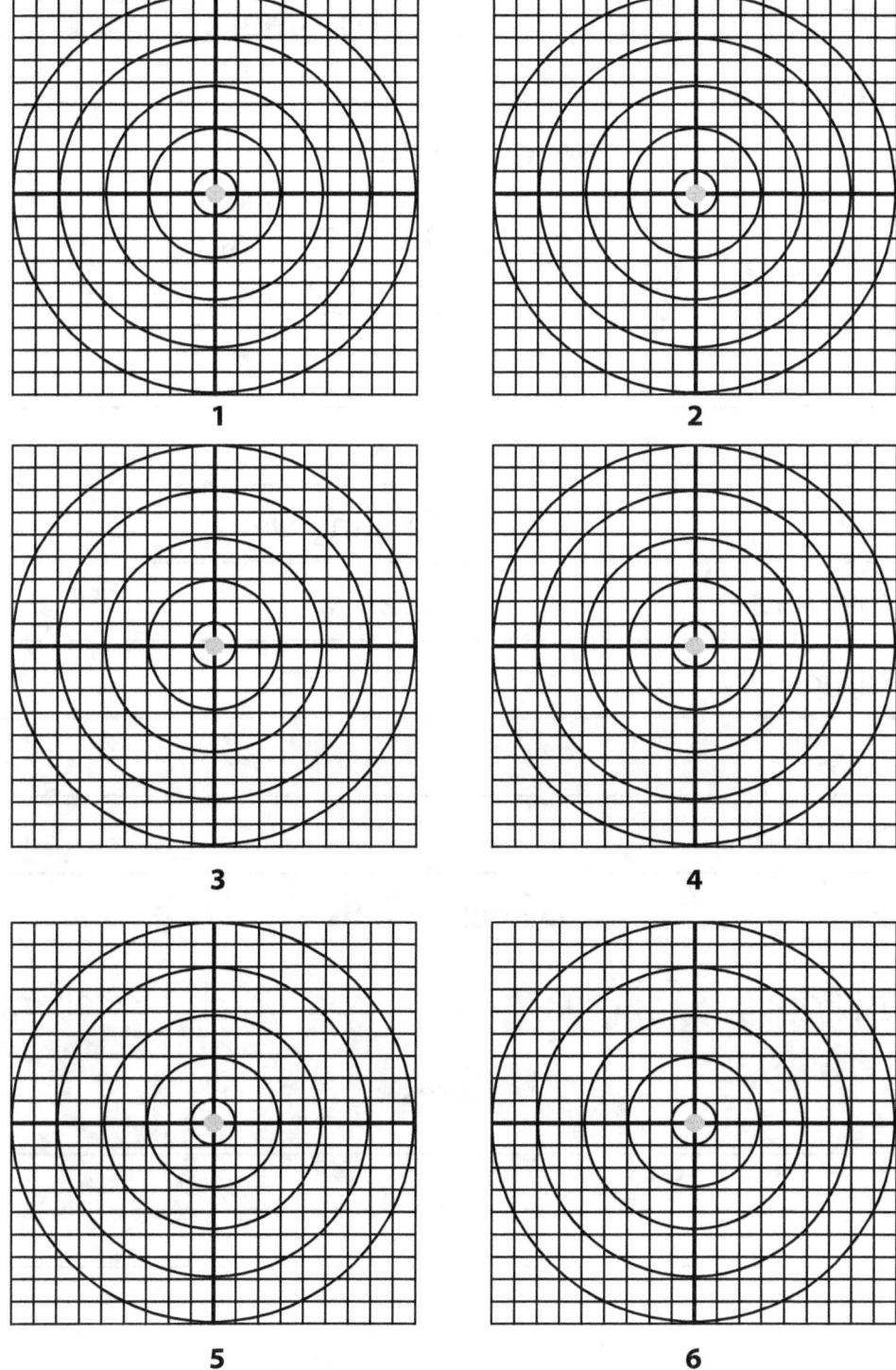

Date: _____ Time: _____

Location: _____

Weather Conditions

☀ ☁ ⛅ 🌦 🌧 🌨 🚩 🌡
☐ ☐ ☐ ☐ ☐ ☐ ____ ____

Firearm:	
Bullet:	Seating Depth:
Powder:	Grains:
Primer:	
Brass:	
Distance:	

Overall Results

☐ Poor   ☐ Fair   ☐ Good   ☐ Excellent

Notes

_____
_____
_____

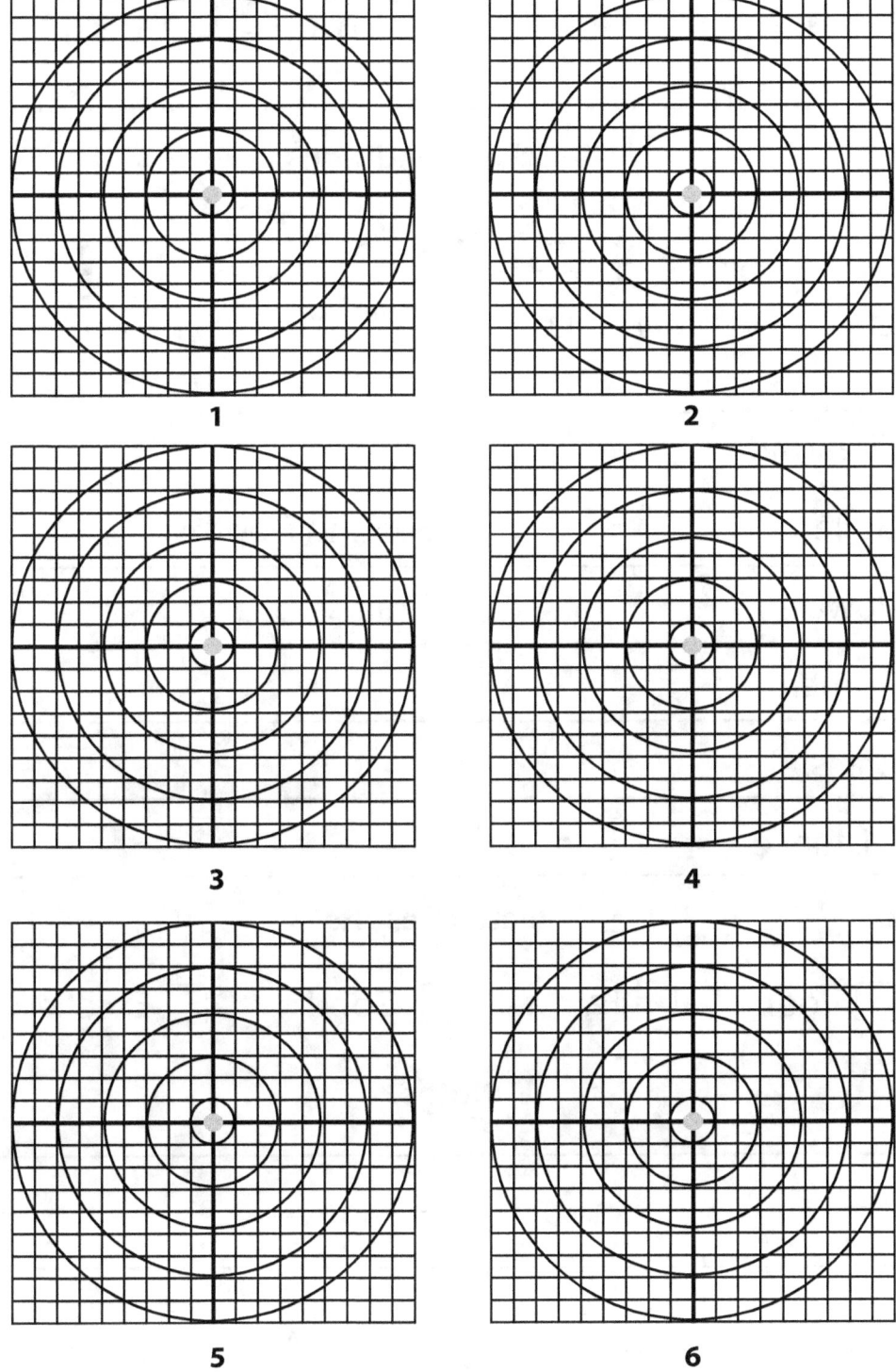

Date: _____ Time: _____

Location: _____

Weather Conditions

☀ ☁ ⛅ 🌧 🌧 🌨 🚩 🌡
☐ ☐ ☐ ☐ ☐ ☐ ___ ___

Firearm:	
Bullet:	Seating Depth:
Powder:	Grains:
Primer:	
Brass:	
Distance:	

Overall Results

☐ Poor   ☐ Fair   ☐ Good   ☐ Excellent

Notes

_____
_____
_____

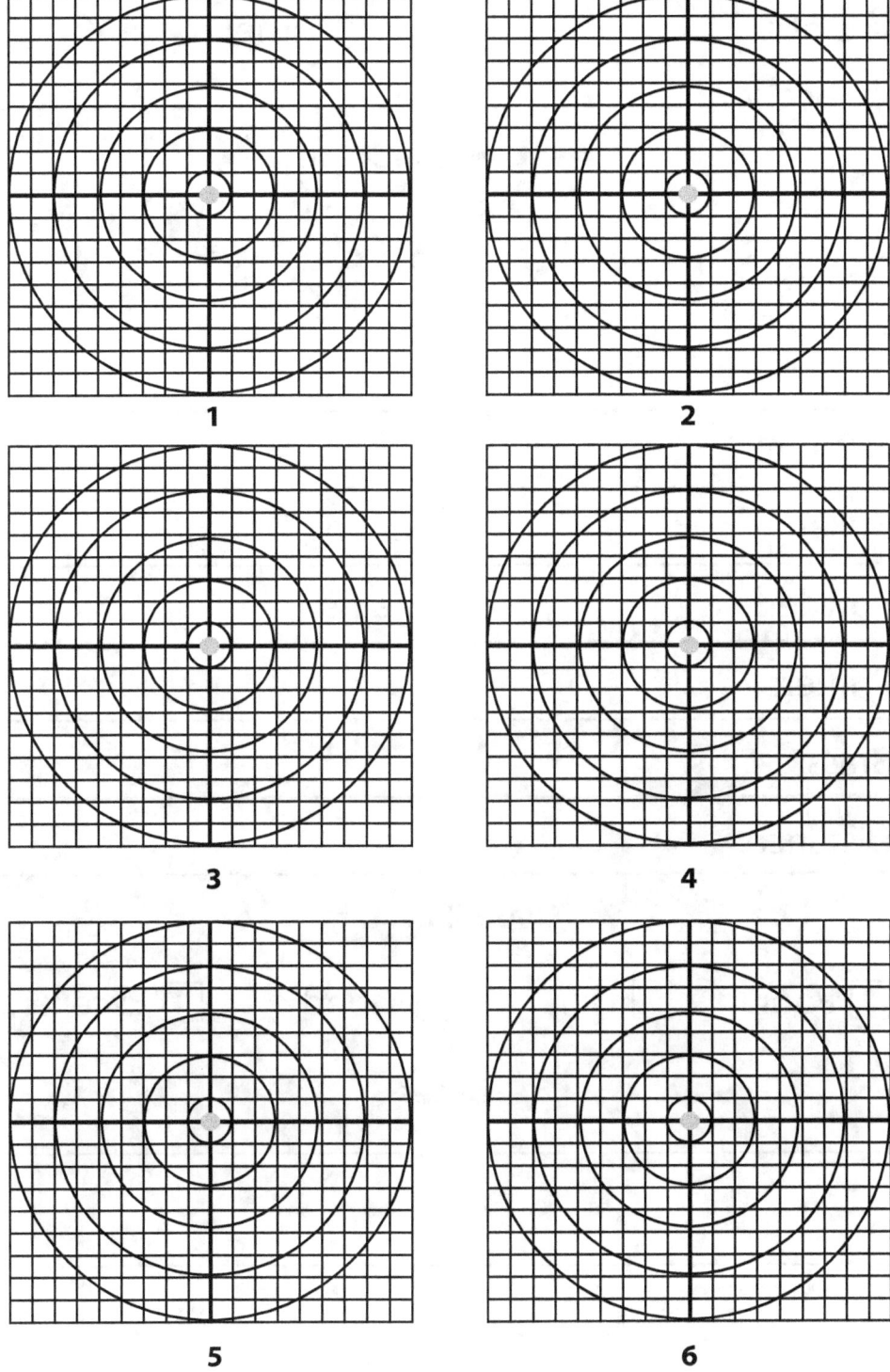

🗓 Date: _____ 🕐 Time: _____

📍 Location: _____

Weather Conditions

☀ ☁ ⛅ 🌧 🌨 🌨 🚩 🌡
☐ ☐ ☐ ☐ ☐ ☐ ___ ___

Firearm:	
Bullet:	Seating Depth:
Powder:	Grains:
Primer:	
Brass:	
Distance:	

Overall Results

☐ Poor   ☐ Fair   ☐ Good   ☐ Excellent

Notes

_____

_____

☆ ☆ ☆ ☆ ☆

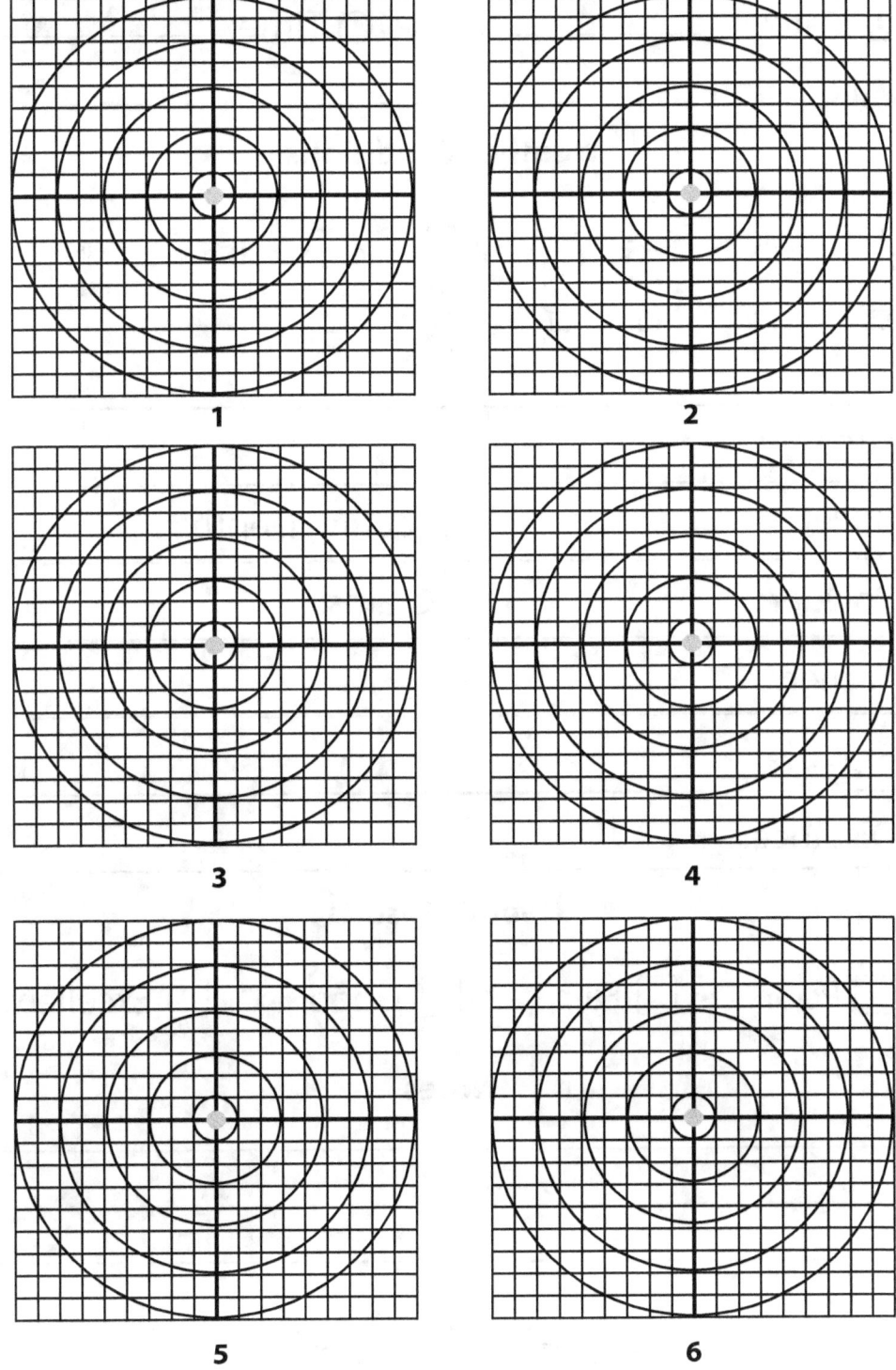

Date: _____   Time: _____

 Location: _____

Weather Conditions

☀ ☁ ⛅ 🌧 🌧 🌨 🚩   🌡
☐   ☐   ☐   ☐   ☐   ☐   _____   _____

Firearm:	
Bullet:	Seating Depth:
Powder:	Grains:
Primer:	
Brass:	
Distance:	

Overall Results

☐ Poor   ☐ Fair   ☐ Good   ☐ Excellent

Notes

_____

_____

_____

☆ ☆ ☆ ☆ ☆

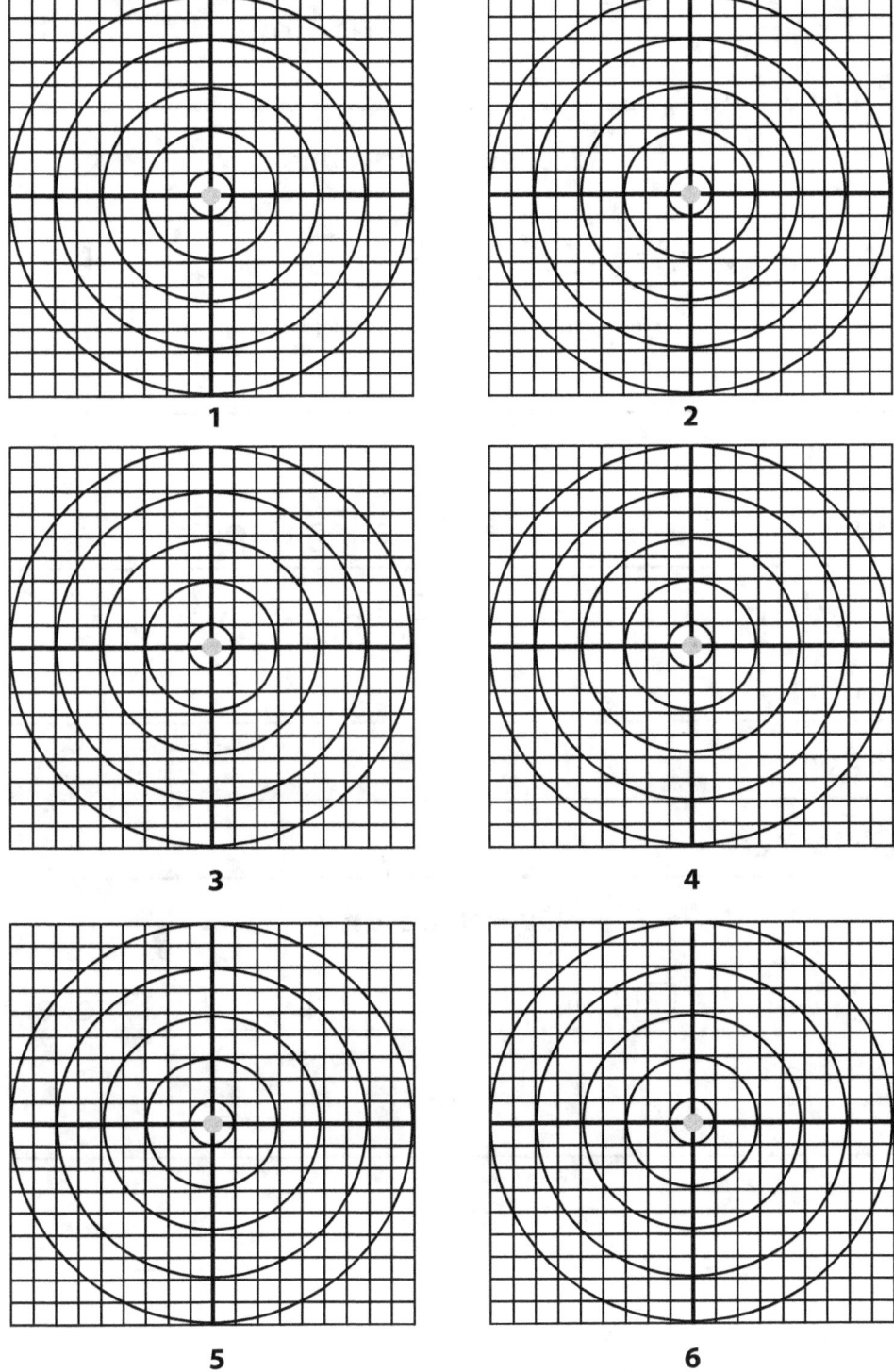

Date: _____ Time: _____

 Location: _____

Weather Conditions

☀ ☐   ☁ ☐   ⛅ ☐   🌦 ☐   🌧 ☐   🌨 ☐   🚩 _____   🌡 _____

Firearm:	
Bullet:	Seating Depth:
Powder:	Grains:
Primer:	
Brass:	
Distance:	

Overall Results

☐ Poor   ☐ Fair   ☐ Good   ☐ Excellent

Notes

_____

_____

_____

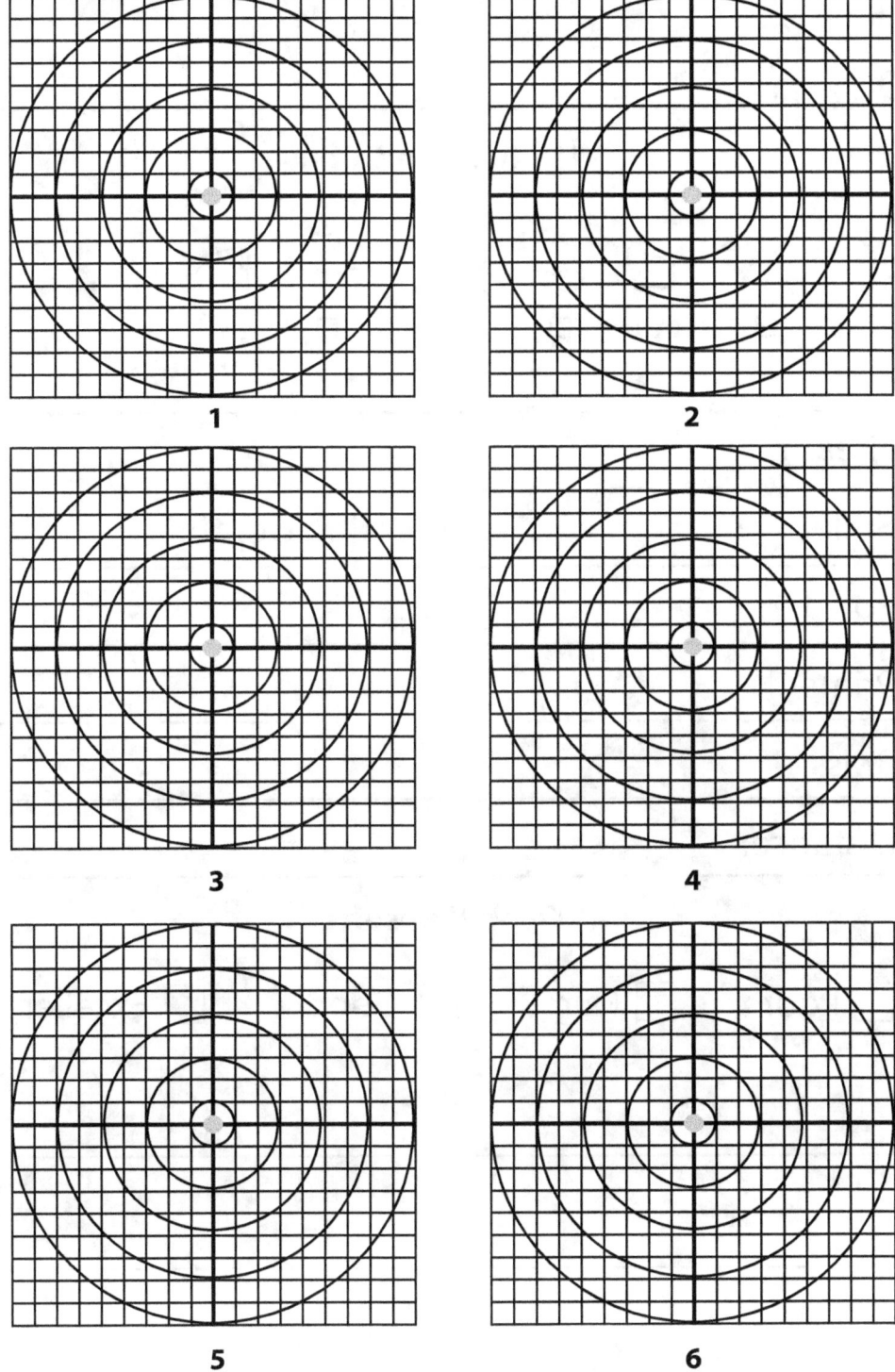

📅 Date: _____ 🕐 Time: _____

📍 Location: _____

Weather Conditions

☀️ ☁️ ⛅ 🌦️ ☁️ 🌨️ 🚩 🌡️
☐   ☐   ☐   ☐   ☐   ☐   _____ _____

Firearm:	
Bullet:	Seating Depth:
Powder:	Grains:
Primer:	
Brass:	
Distance:	

Overall Results

☐ Poor   ☐ Fair   ☐ Good   ☐ Excellent

Notes

_____

_____

_____

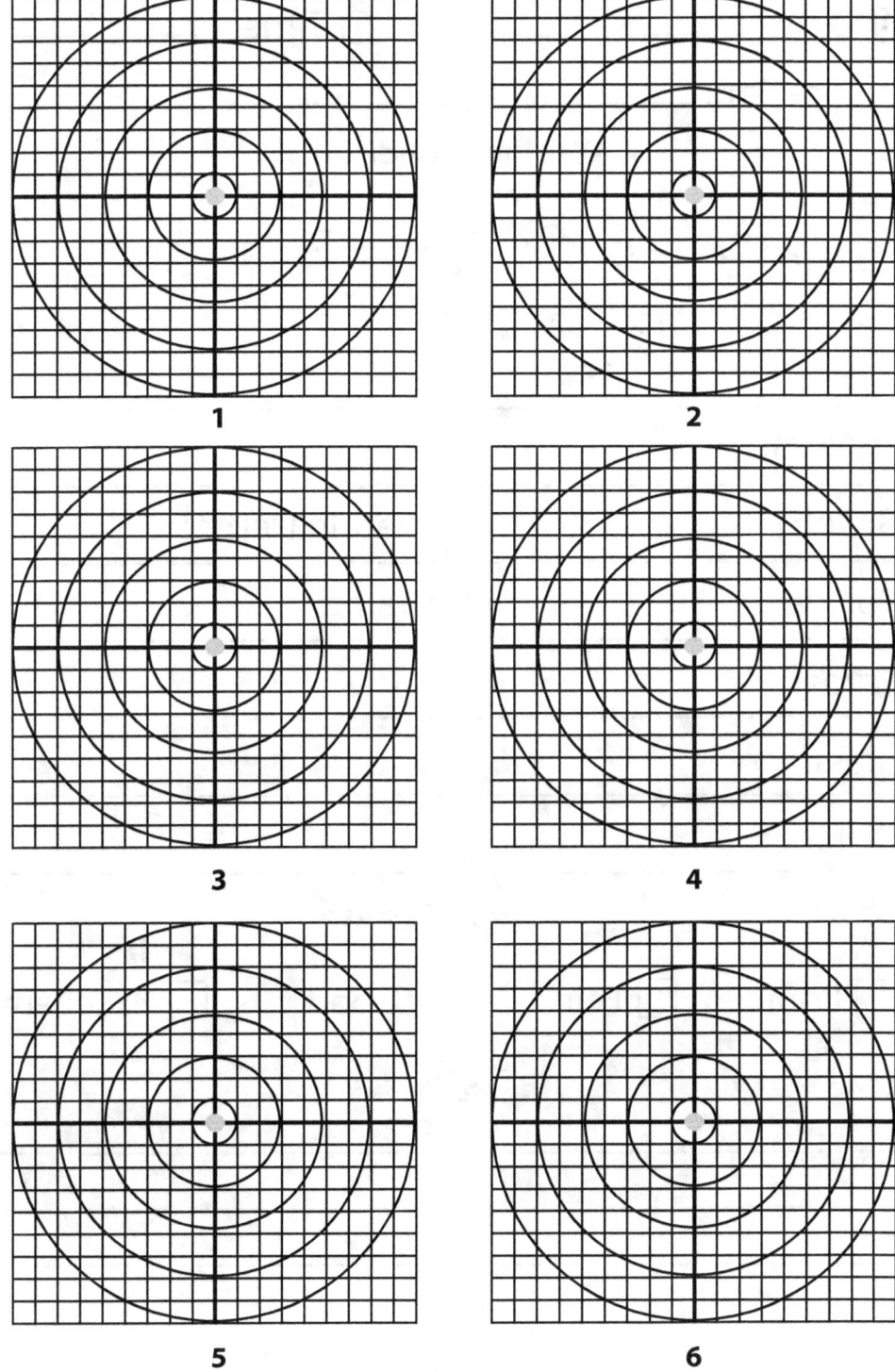

Date: _____ Time: _____

Location: _____

Weather Conditions

☐ ☐ ☐ ☐ ☐ ☐ ☐ _____

Firearm:	
Bullet:	Seating Depth:
Powder:	Grains:
Primer:	
Brass:	
Distance:	

Overall Results

☐ Poor ☐ Fair ☐ Good ☐ Excellent

Notes

_____
_____
_____

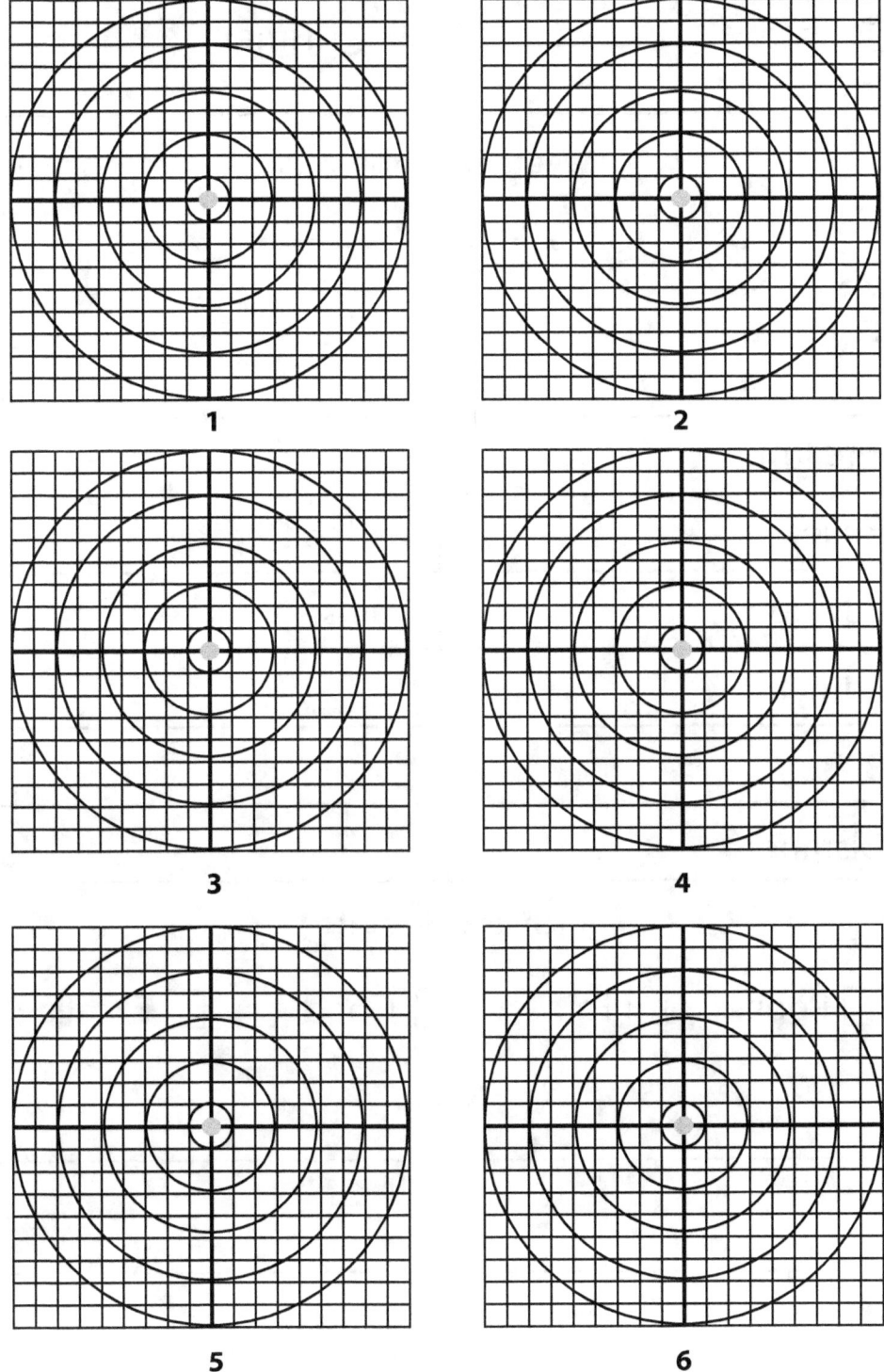

Date: _____ Time: _____

Location: _____

Weather Conditions

☀ ☁ ⛅ 🌦 🌧 🌨 🚩 🌡
☐ ☐ ☐ ☐ ☐ ☐ _____ _____

Firearm:	
Bullet:	Seating Depth:
Powder:	Grains:
Primer:	
Brass:	
Distance:	

Overall Results

☐ Poor   ☐ Fair   ☐ Good   ☐ Excellent

Notes

_____
_____
_____

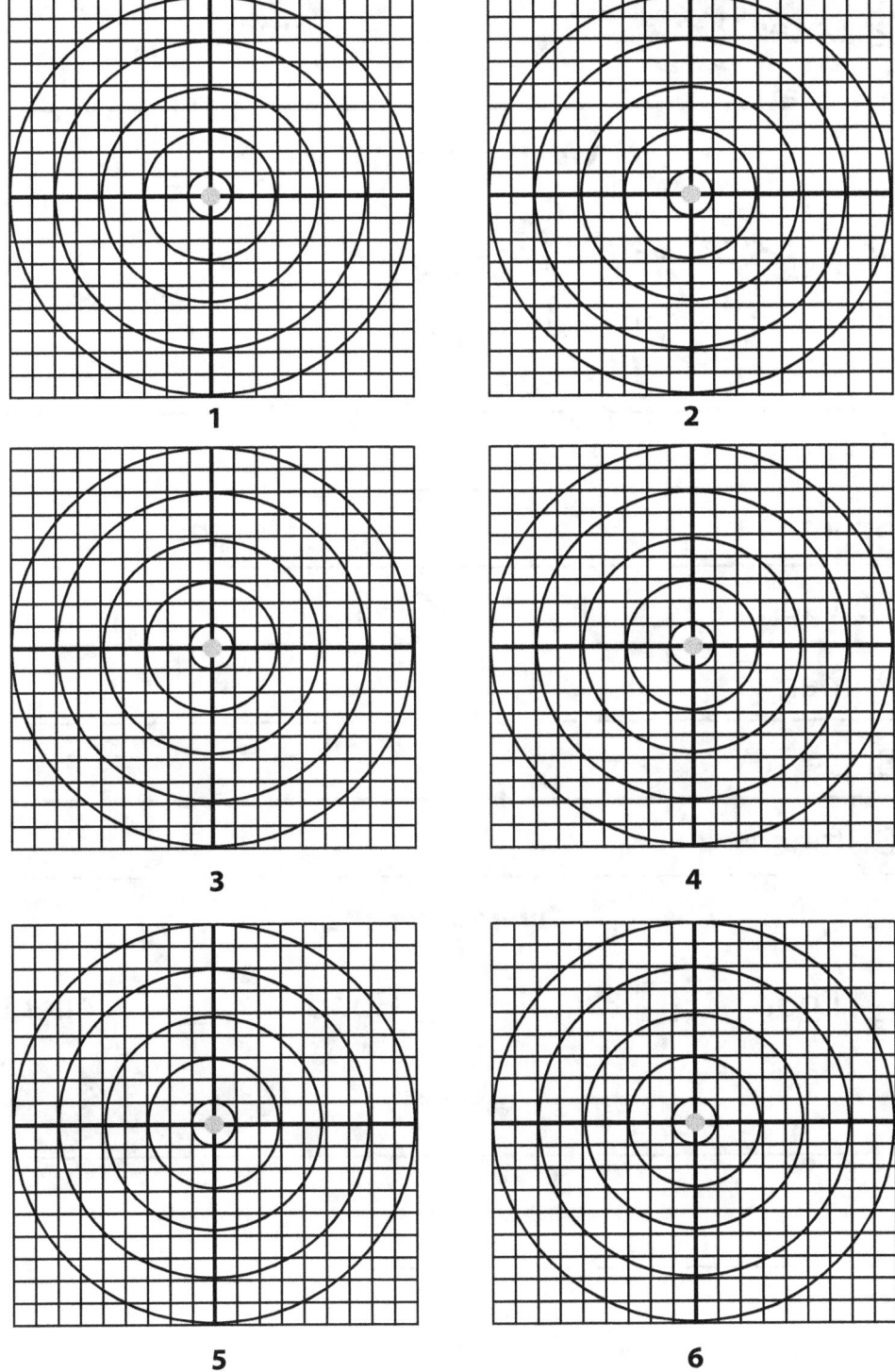

📅 Date: _____ 🕐 Time: _____

📍 Location: _____

Weather Conditions

☀️ ☁️ ⛅ 🌧️ 🌧️ 🌨️ 🚩 🌡️
☐ ☐ ☐ ☐ ☐ ☐   ___ ___

Firearm:	
Bullet:	Seating Depth:
Powder:	Grains:
Primer:	
Brass:	
Distance:	

Overall Results

☐ Poor   ☐ Fair   ☐ Good   ☐ Excellent

Notes

_____
_____
_____

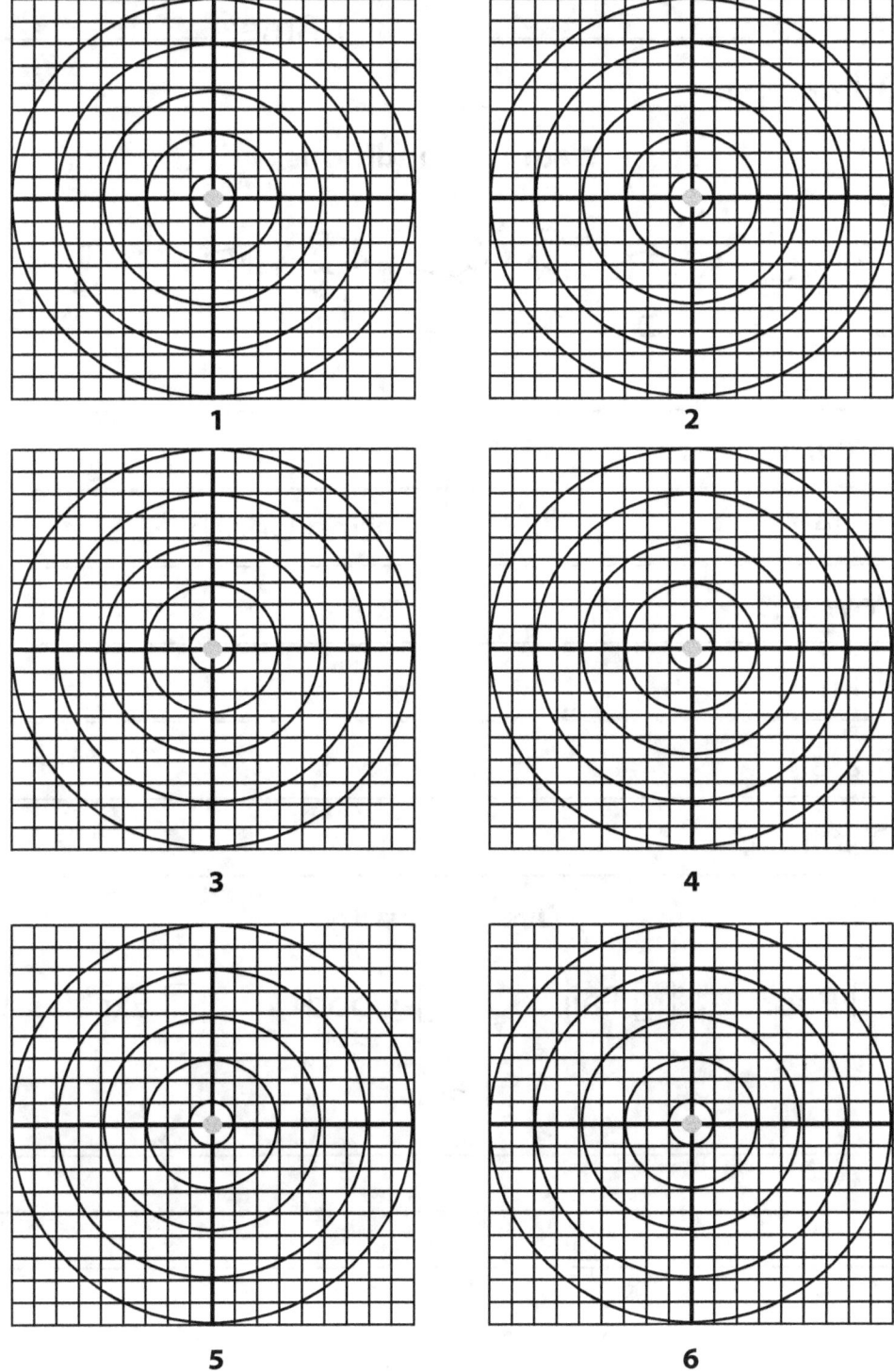

Date: _____ Time: _____
Location: _____

Weather Conditions

☀ ☁ 🌤 🌧 🌧 🌨 🚩 🌡
☐ ☐ ☐ ☐ ☐ ☐ ___ ___

Firearm:	
Bullet:	Seating Depth:
Powder:	Grains:
Primer:	
Brass:	
Distance:	

Overall Results

☐ Poor   ☐ Fair   ☐ Good   ☐ Excellent

Notes

_____
_____
_____

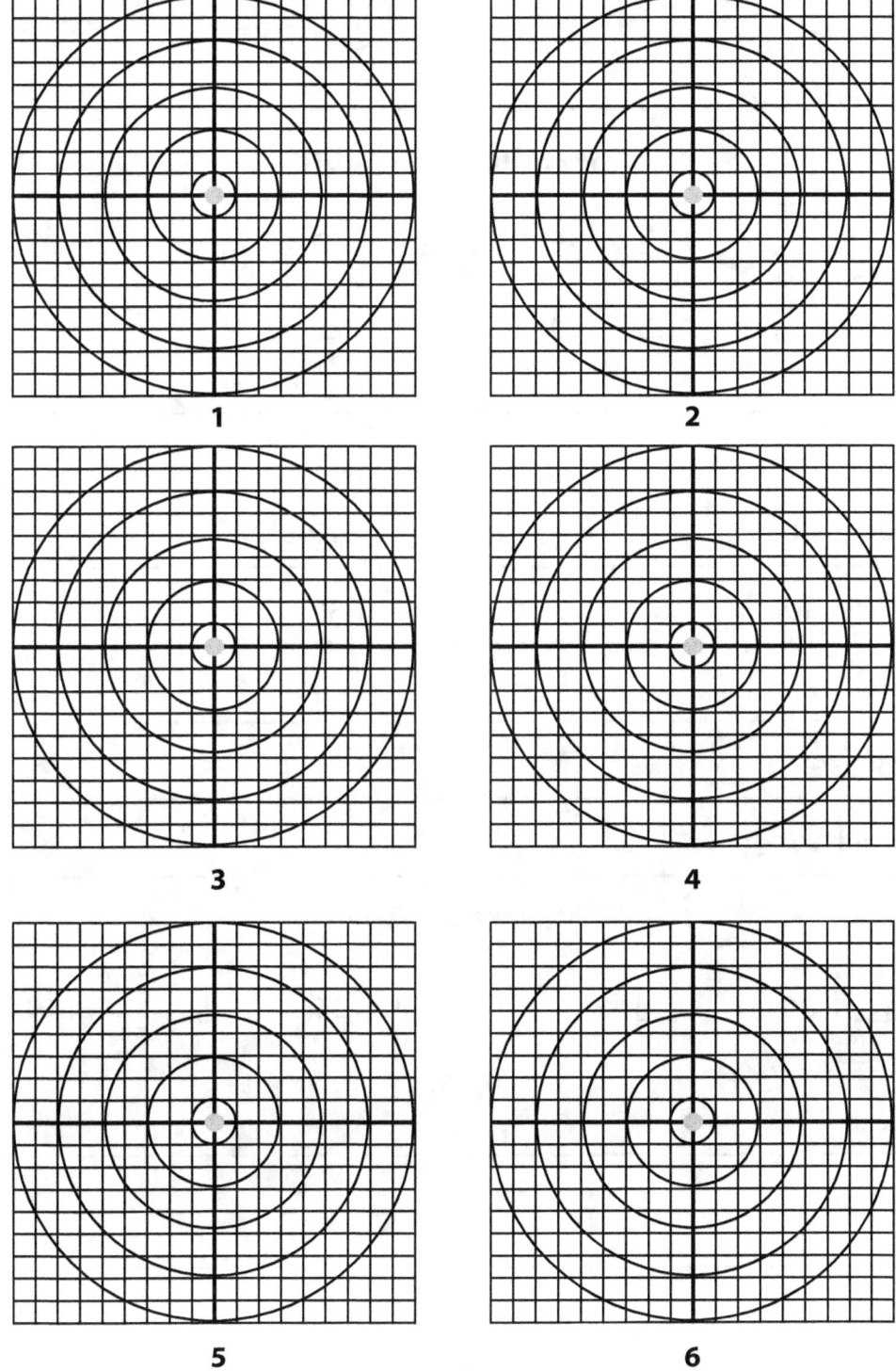

📅 Date: _____ 🕐 Time: _____

📍 Location: _____

Weather Conditions

☀️ ☁️ ⛅ 🌧️ 🌧️ 🌨️ 🚩 🌡️
☐   ☐   ☐   ☐   ☐   ☐   _____ _____

Firearm:	
Bullet:	Seating Depth:
Powder:	Grains:
Primer:	
Brass:	
Distance:	

Overall Results

☐ Poor   ☐ Fair   ☐ Good   ☐ Excellent

Notes

_____
_____
_____

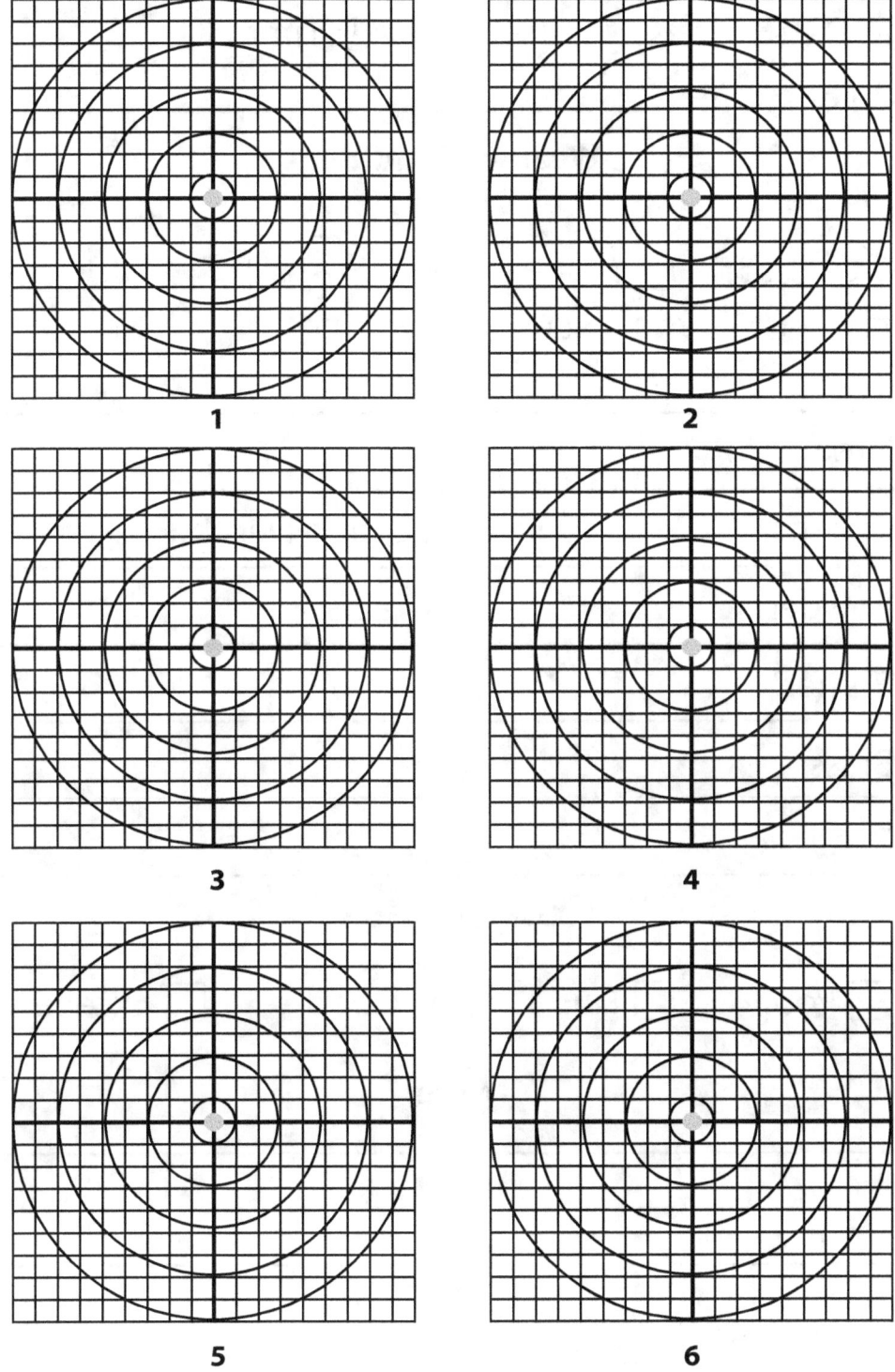

Date: _____ Time: _____

 Location: _____

Weather Conditions

☀ ☐   ⛅ ☐   🌤 ☐   🌧 ☐   🌧 ☐   🌨 ☐   🚩 _____   🌡 _____

Firearm:	
Bullet:	Seating Depth:
Powder:	Grains:
Primer:	
Brass:	
Distance:	

Overall Results

☐ Poor   ☐ Fair   ☐ Good   ☐ Excellent

Notes

_____

_____

_____

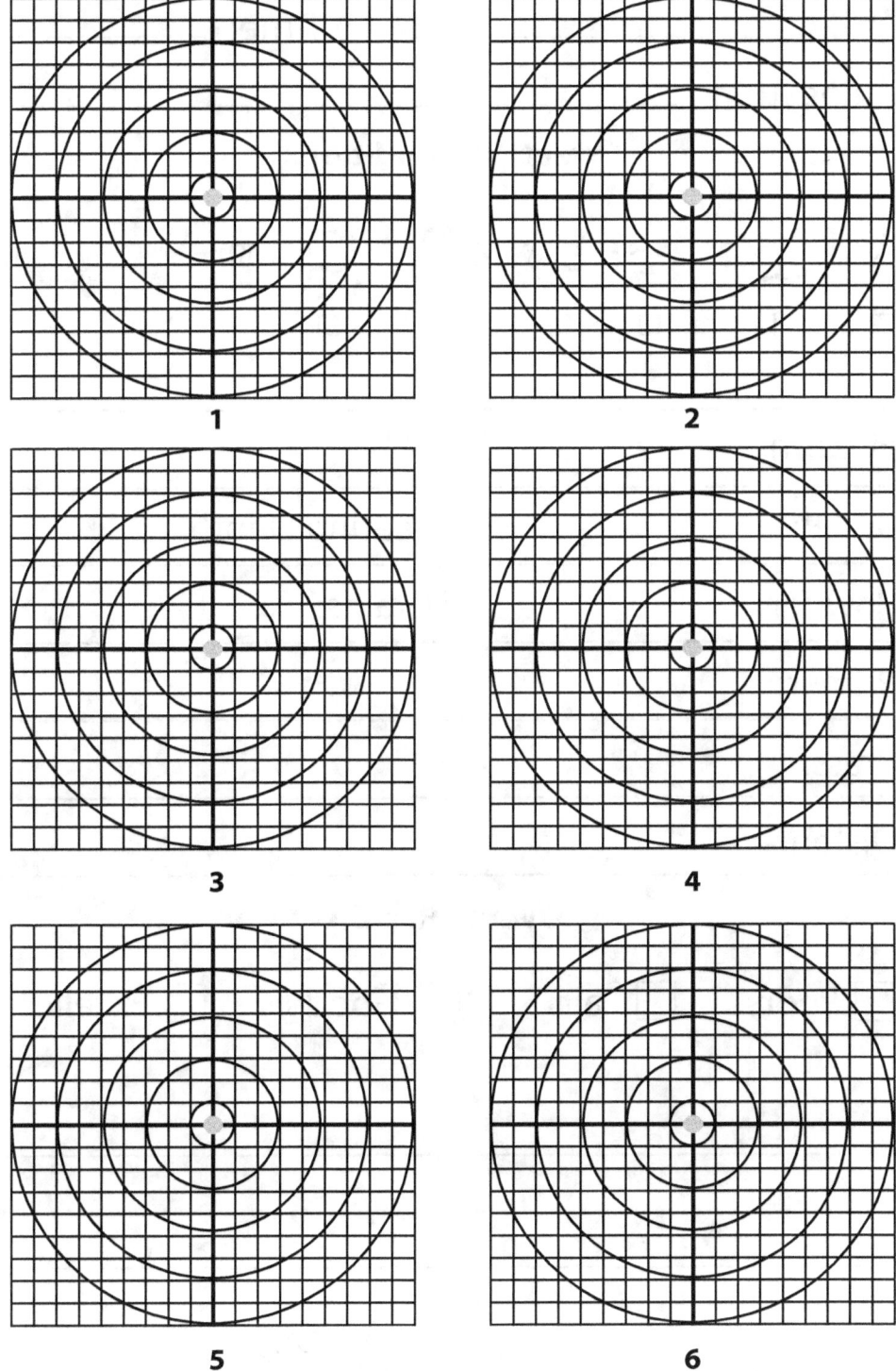

📅 Date: _____ 🕐 Time: _____

📍 Location: _____

Weather Conditions

☀ ☁ ⛅ 🌧 🌧 🌨 🚩 🌡
☐ ☐ ☐ ☐ ☐ ☐

Firearm:	
Bullet:	Seating Depth:
Powder:	Grains:
Primer:	
Brass:	
Distance:	

Overall Results

☐ Poor   ☐ Fair   ☐ Good   ☐ Excellent

Notes

_____
_____
_____

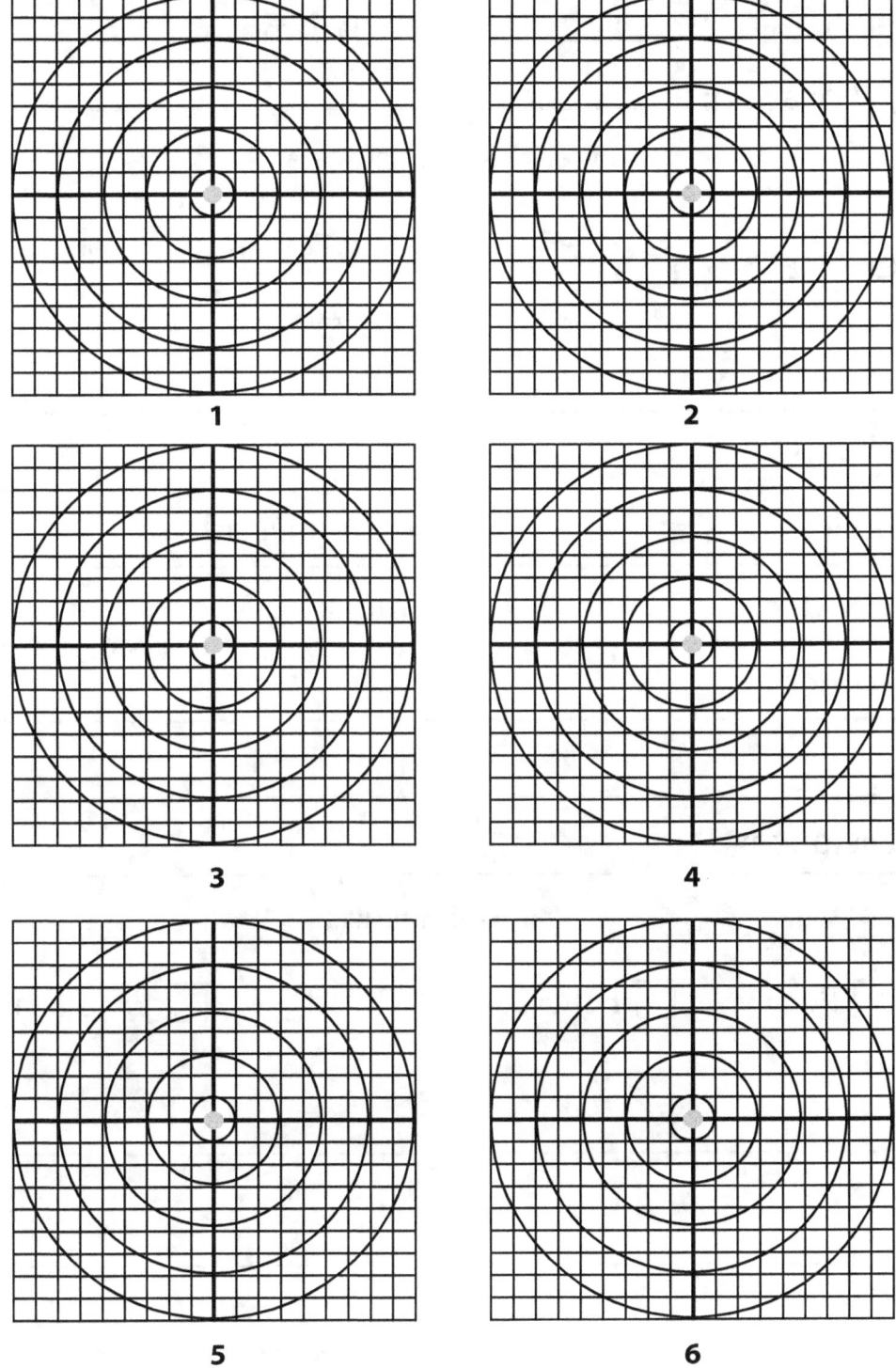

Date: _____ Time: _____

Location: _____

Weather Conditions

☀ ☁ ⛅ 🌧 🌧 🌨 🚩 🌡
☐ ☐ ☐ ☐ ☐ ☐ _____ _____

Firearm:	
Bullet:	Seating Depth:
Powder:	Grains:
Primer:	
Brass:	
Distance:	

Overall Results

☐ Poor   ☐ Fair   ☐ Good   ☐ Excellent

Notes

_____
_____
_____

☆ ☆ ☆ ☆ ☆

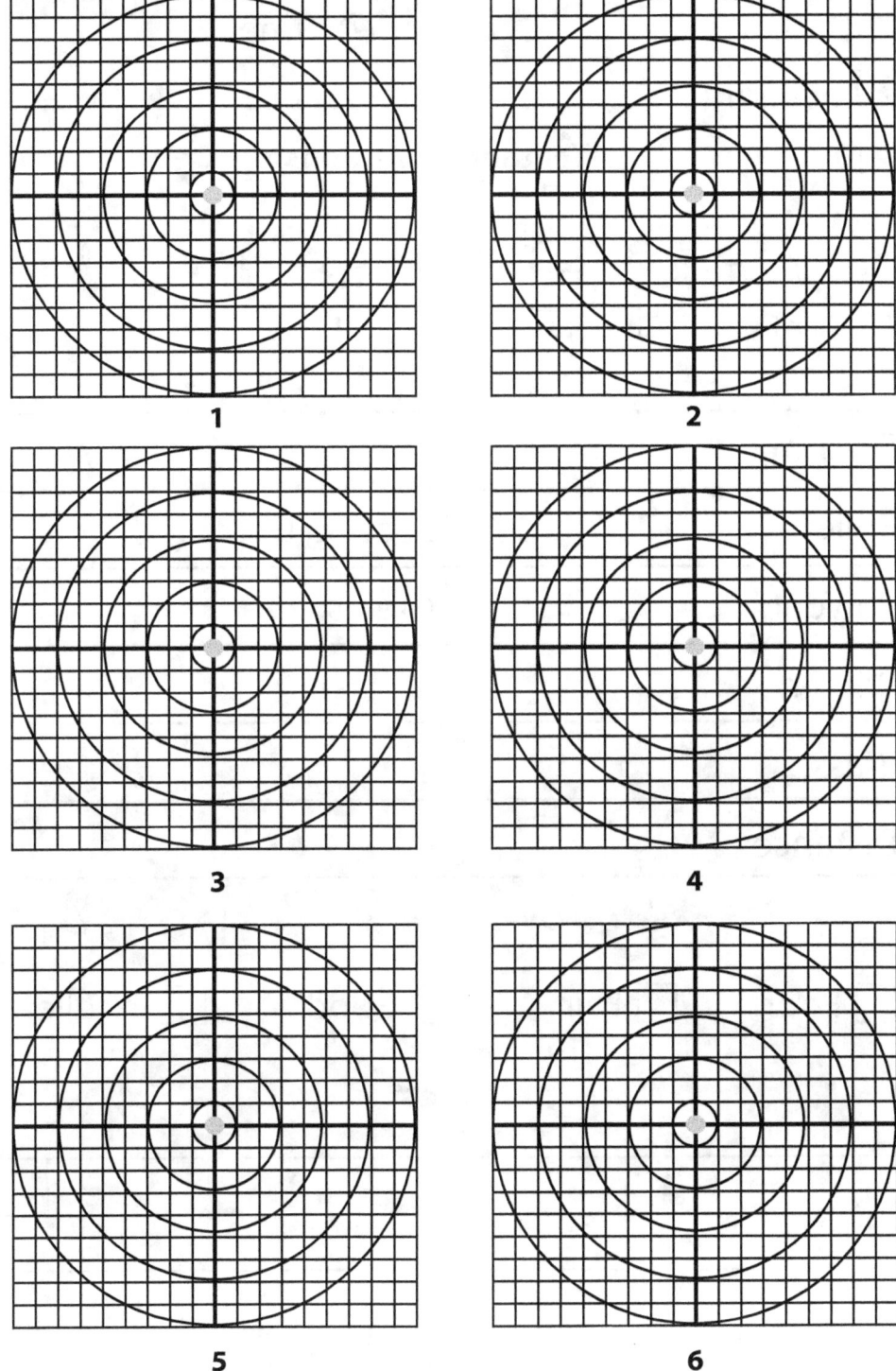

🗓 Date: _____ 🕐 Time: _____

📍 Location: _____

Weather Conditions

☀ ☁ ⛅ 🌦 🌧 🌨 🚩 🌡
☐ ☐ ☐ ☐ ☐ ☐ _____ _____

Firearm:	
Bullet:	Seating Depth:
Powder:	Grains:
Primer:	
Brass:	
Distance:	

Overall Results

☐ Poor   ☐ Fair   ☐ Good   ☐ Excellent

Notes

_____
_____
_____

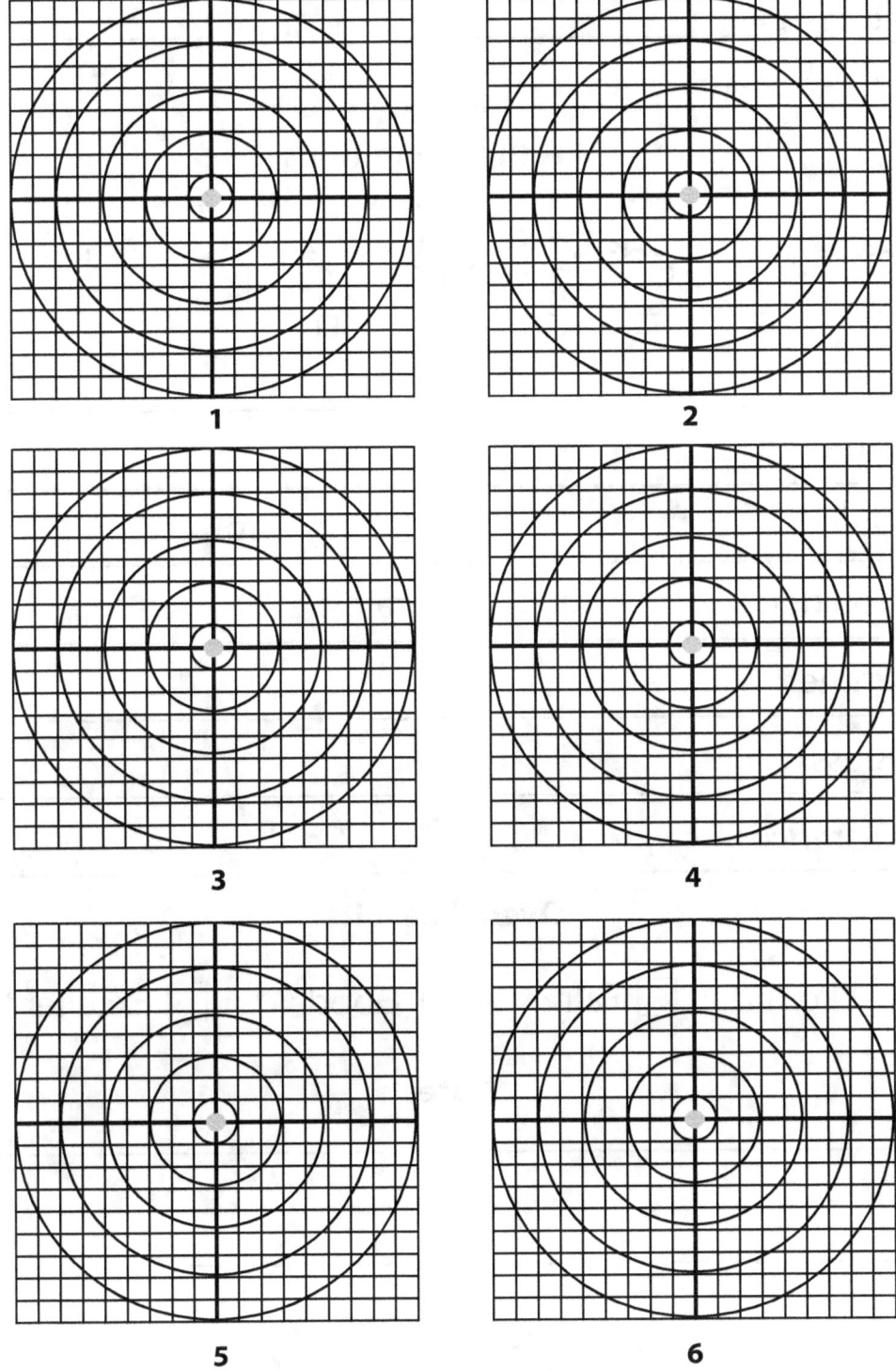

Date: _____ Time: _____

Location: _____

Weather Conditions

☀ ☁ ⛅ 🌦 🌧 🌨 🚩 🌡
☐ ☐ ☐ ☐ ☐ ☐ _____ _____

Firearm:	
Bullet:	Seating Depth:
Powder:	Grains:
Primer:	
Brass:	
Distance:	

Overall Results

☐ Poor   ☐ Fair   ☐ Good   ☐ Excellent

Notes

_____

_____

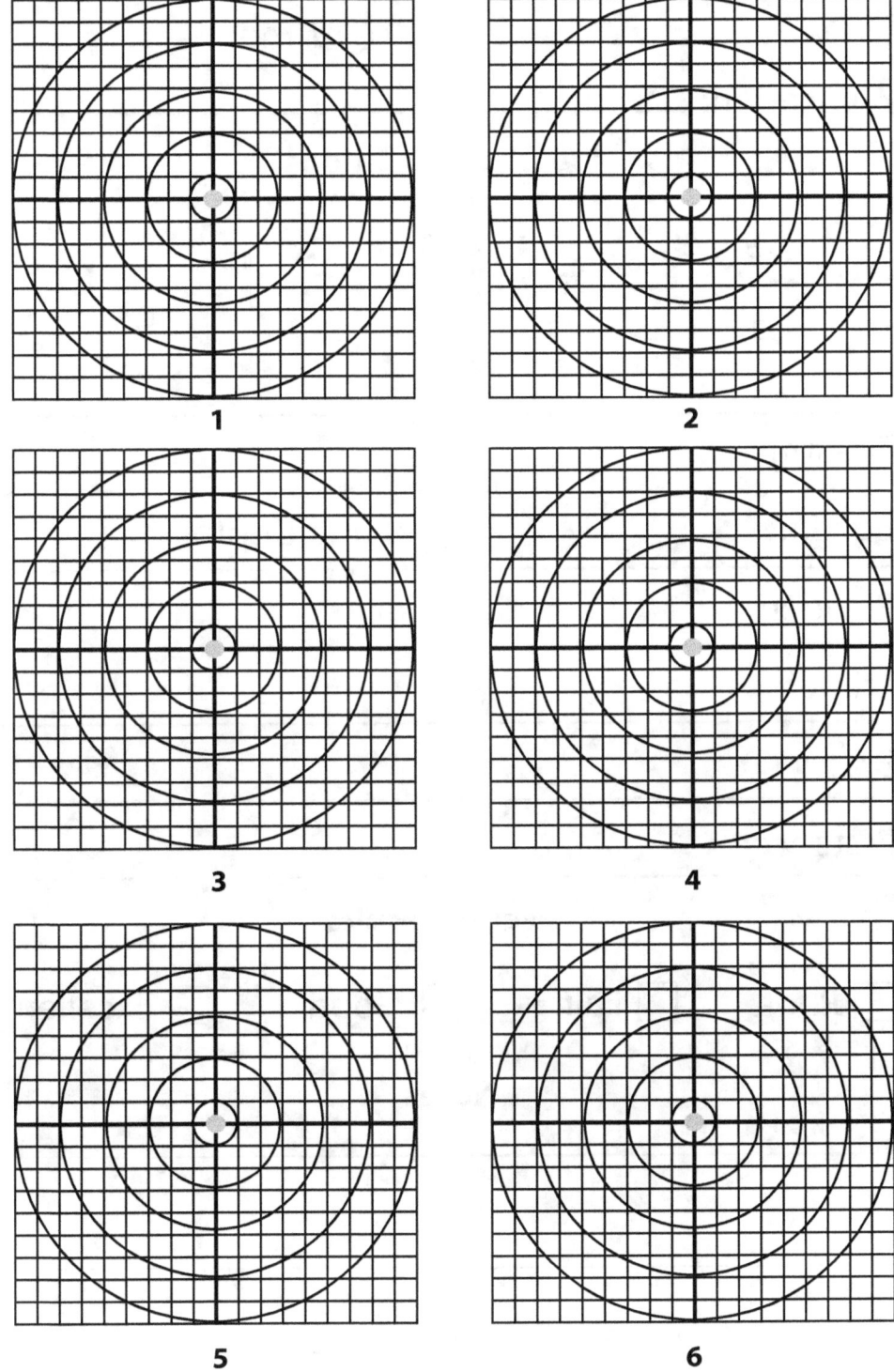

📅 Date: _____   🕐 Time: _____

📍 Location: _____

Weather Conditions

☀ ☁ ⛅ 🌧 🌧 🌨 🚩 🌡
☐ ☐ ☐ ☐ ☐ ☐ _____ _____

Firearm:	
Bullet:	Seating Depth:
Powder:	Grains:
Primer:	
Brass:	
Distance:	

Overall Results

☐ Poor   ☐ Fair   ☐ Good   ☐ Excellent

Notes

_____

_____

_____

☆ ☆ ☆ ☆ ☆

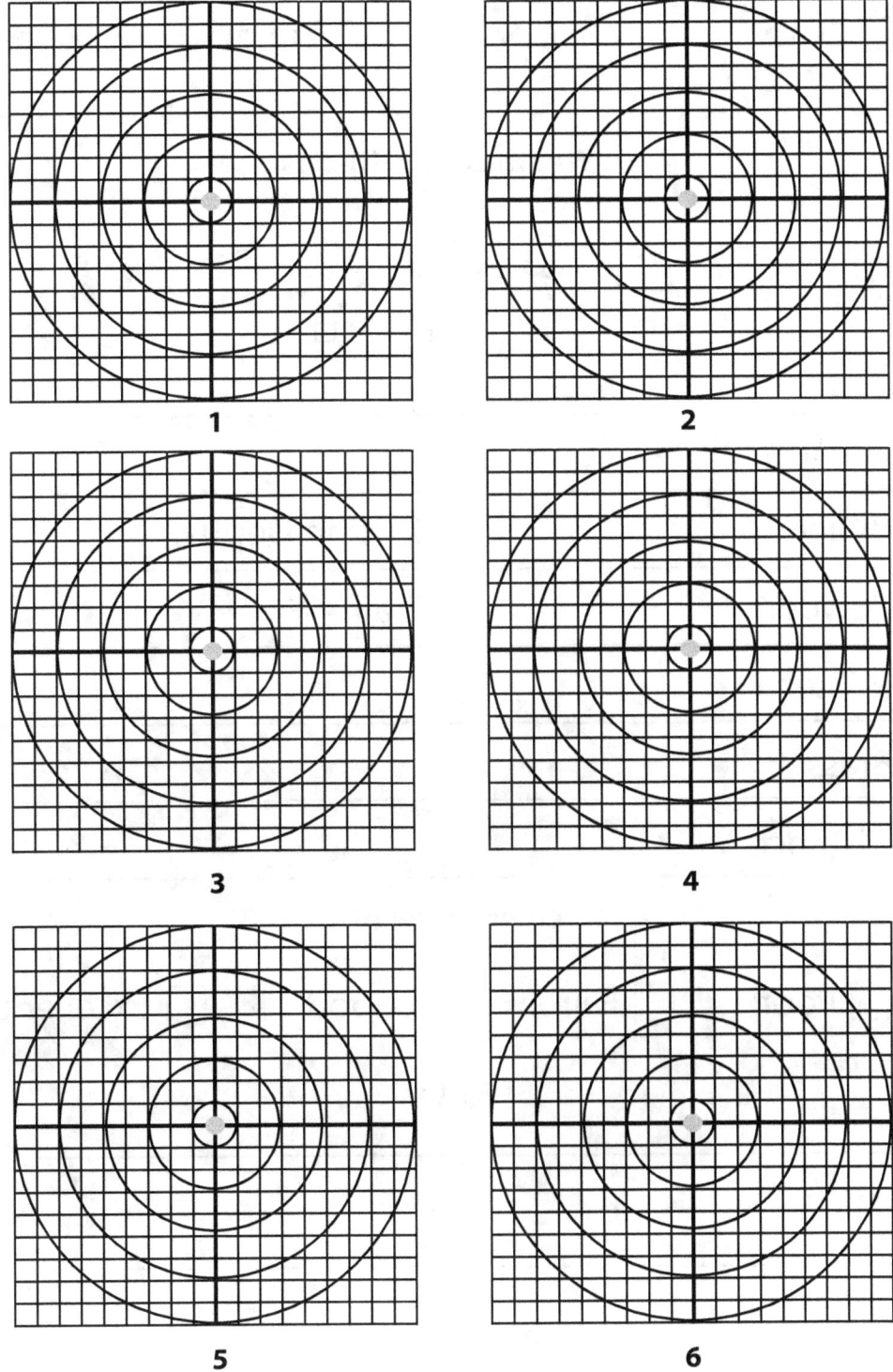

Date: _____ Time: _____
Location: _____

Weather Conditions

☀ ☁ ⛅ 🌧 🌧 🌨 🚩 🌡
☐ ☐ ☐ ☐ ☐ ☐ _____ _____

Firearm:	
Bullet:	Seating Depth:
Powder:	Grains:
Primer:	
Brass:	
Distance:	

Overall Results

☐ Poor   ☐ Fair   ☐ Good   ☐ Excellent

Notes
_____
_____
_____

☆ ☆ ☆ ☆ ☆

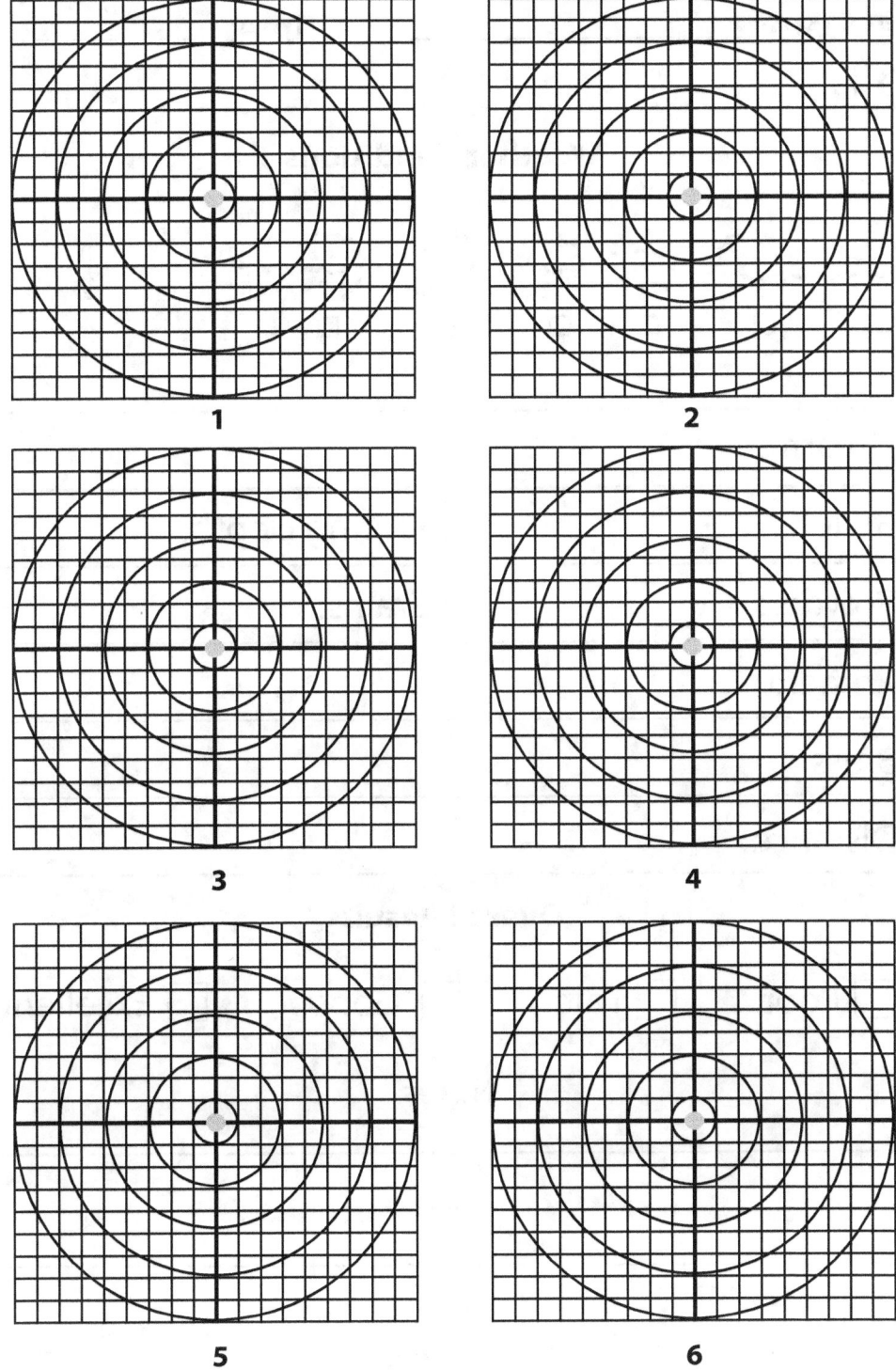

Date: _____ Time: _____

 Location: _____

Weather Conditions

☀ ☁ ⛅ 🌦 🌧 🌨 🚩 🌡
☐ ☐ ☐ ☐ ☐ ☐ _____ _____

Firearm:	
Bullet:	Seating Depth:
Powder:	Grains:
Primer:	
Brass:	
Distance:	

Overall Results

☐ Poor   ☐ Fair   ☐ Good   ☐ Excellent

Notes

_____
_____
_____

☆ ☆ ☆ ☆ ☆

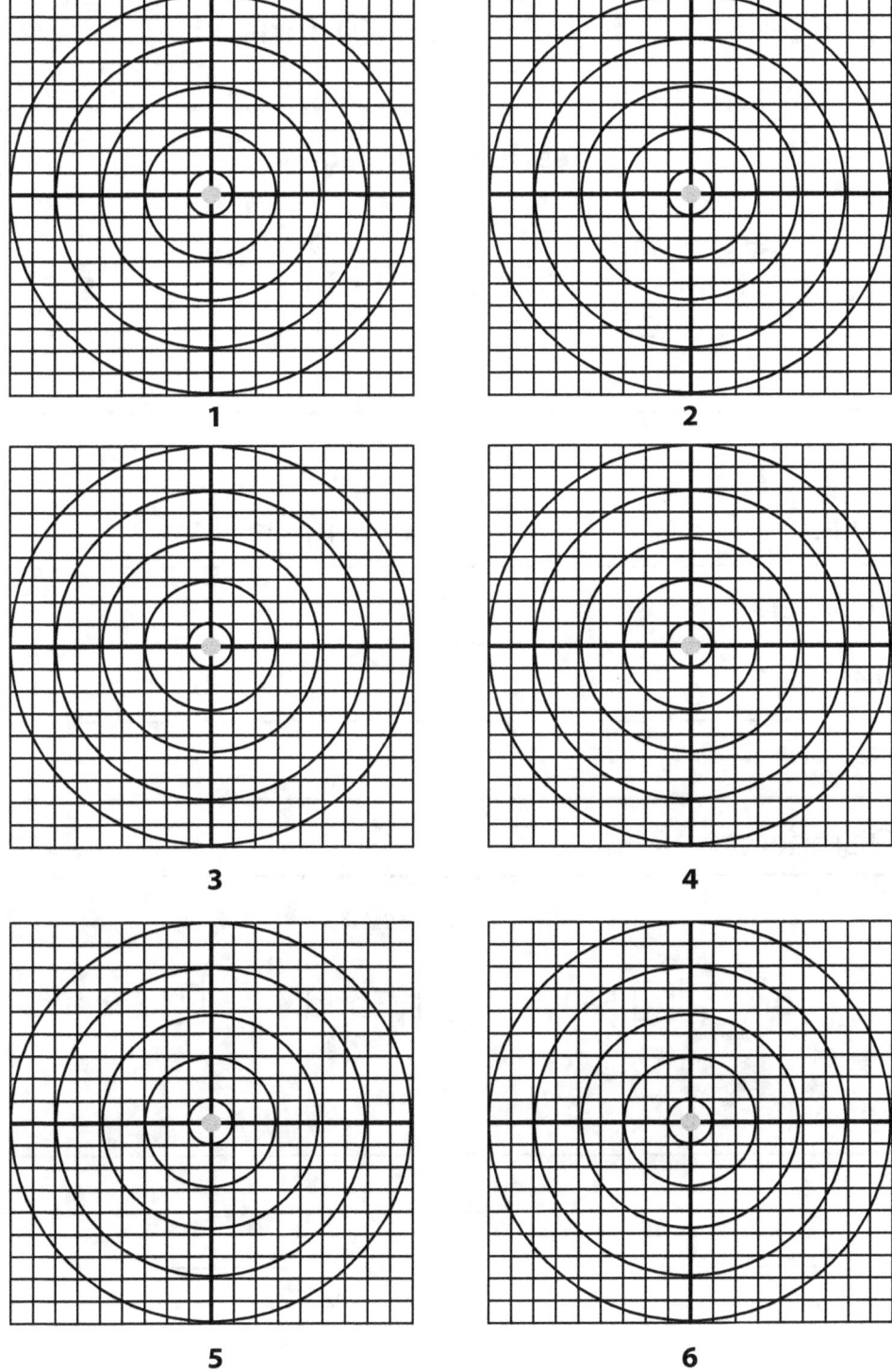

Date: _____ Time: _____

Location: _____

Weather Conditions

☀ ☁ ⛅ 🌧 🌧 🌨 🚩 🌡
☐ ☐ ☐ ☐ ☐ ☐ ___ ___

Firearm:	
Bullet:	Seating Depth:
Powder:	Grains:
Primer:	
Brass:	
Distance:	

Overall Results

☐ Poor ☐ Fair ☐ Good ☐ Excellent

Notes

_____
_____
_____

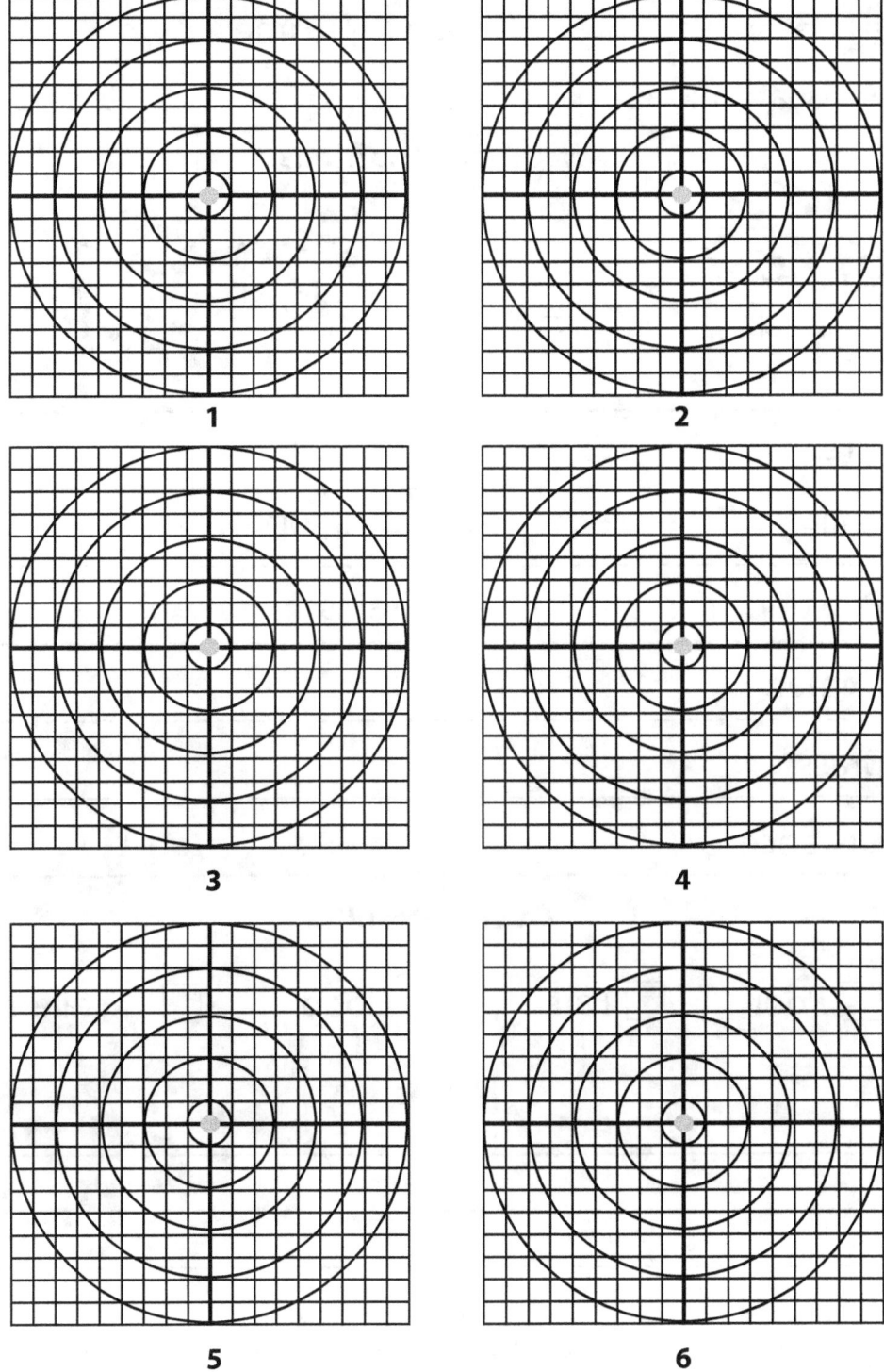

📅 Date: _____ 🕐 Time: _____

📍 Location: _____

Weather Conditions

☀️ ☁️ ⛅ 🌧️ 🌨️ 🌨️ 🚩 _____ 🌡️ _____

☐   ☐   ☐   ☐   ☐   ☐

Firearm:	
Bullet:	Seating Depth:
Powder:	Grains:
Primer:	
Brass:	
Distance:	

Overall Results

☐ Poor   ☐ Fair   ☐ Good   ☐ Excellent

Notes

_____

_____

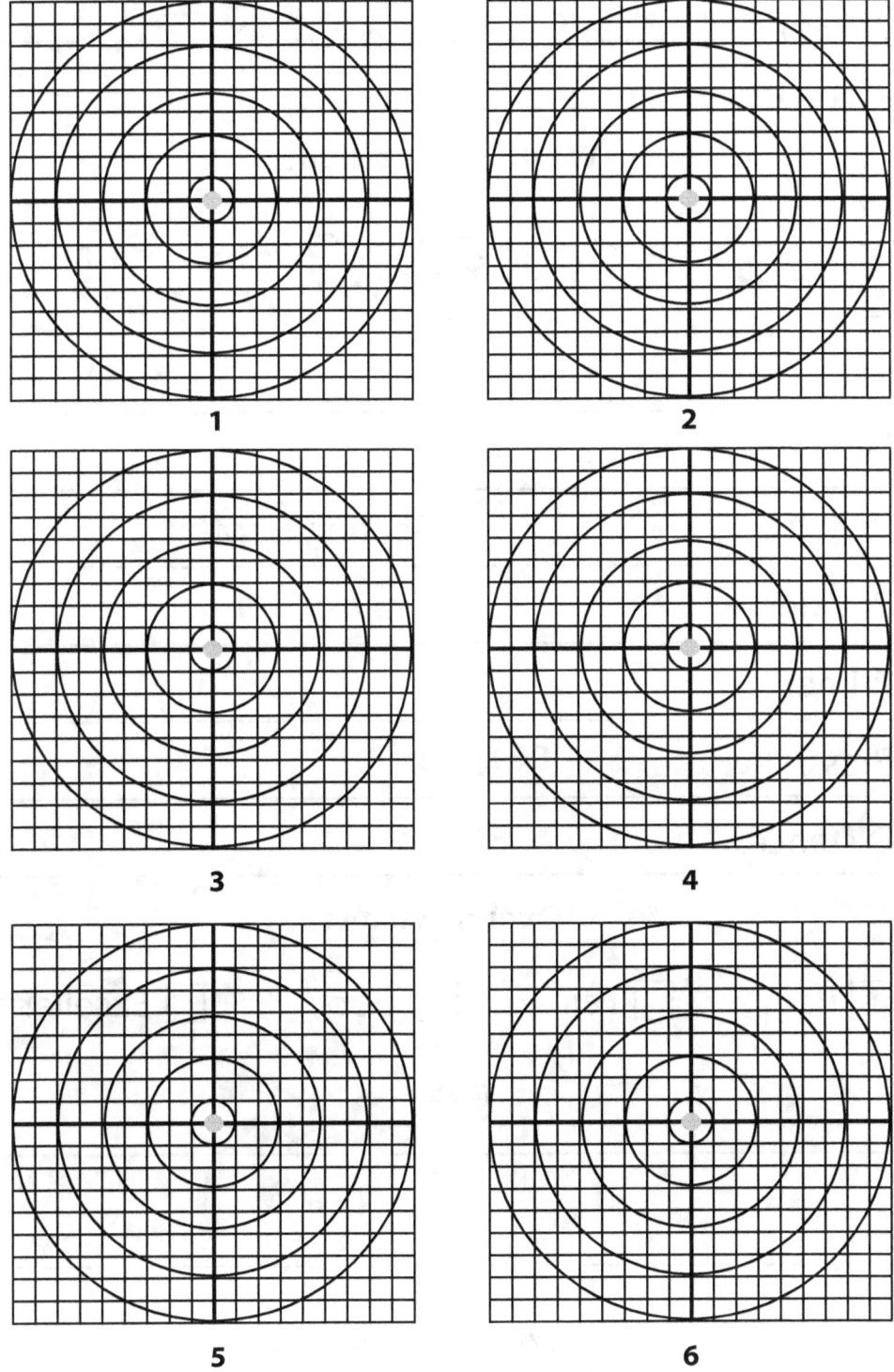

Date: _____   Time: _____

Location: _____

Weather Conditions

☀ ☁ ⛅ 🌦 🌧 🌨 🚩 🌡
☐ ☐ ☐ ☐ ☐ ☐ _____ _____

Firearm:	
Bullet:	Seating Depth:
Powder:	Grains:
Primer:	
Brass:	
Distance:	

Overall Results

☐ Poor   ☐ Fair   ☐ Good   ☐ Excellent

Notes

_____

_____

_____

☆ ☆ ☆ ☆ ☆

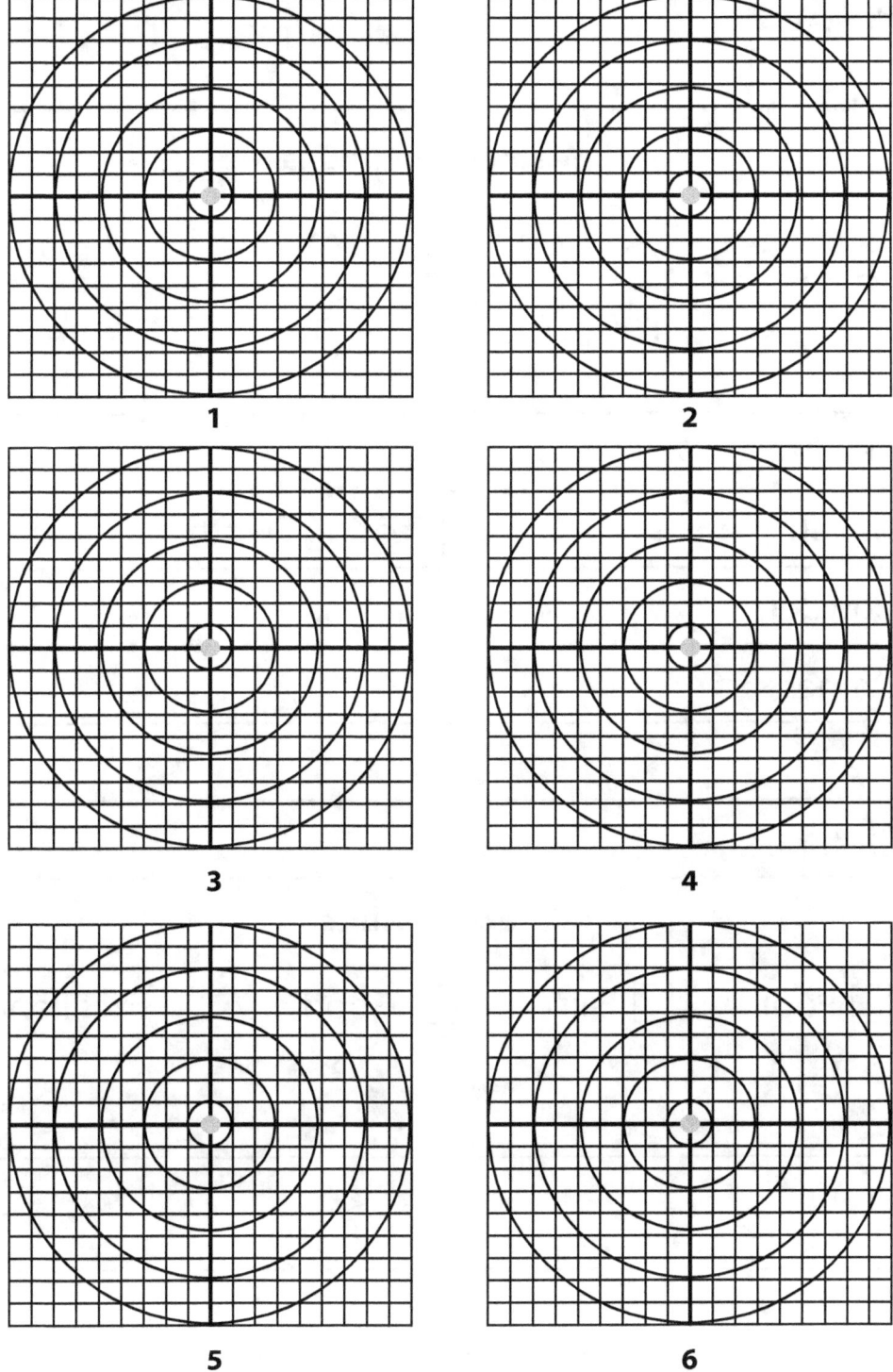

Date: _____   Time: _____

 Location: _____

Weather Conditions

☀ ☁ ⛅ 🌧 🌧 🌨 🚩 🌡
☐   ☐   ☐   ☐   ☐   ☐   _____   _____

Firearm:	
Bullet:	Seating Depth:
Powder:	Grains:
Primer:	
Brass:	
Distance:	

Overall Results

☐ Poor   ☐ Fair   ☐ Good   ☐ Excellent

Notes

_____
_____
_____

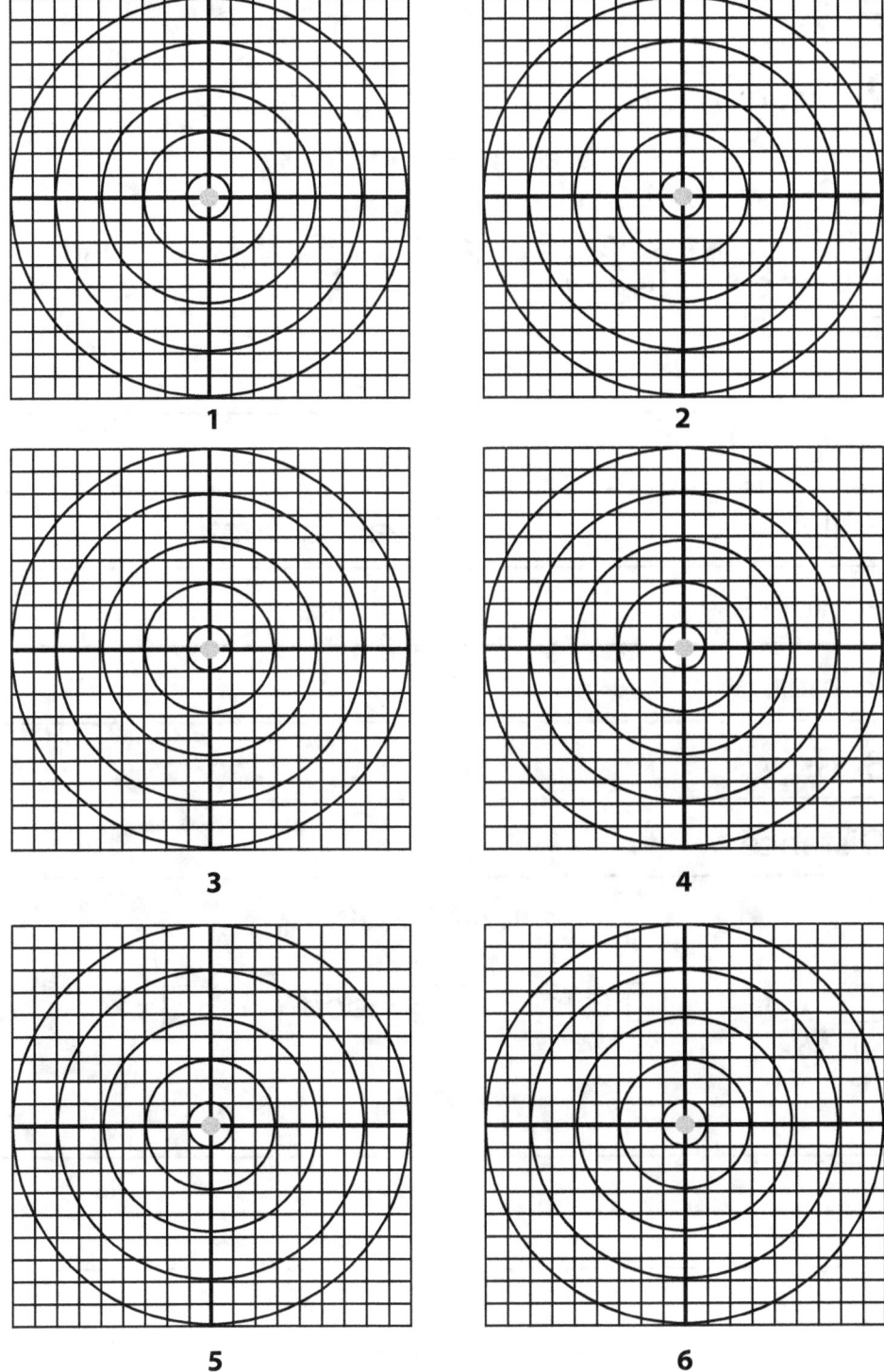

Date: _____ Time: _____

Location: _____

Weather Conditions

☀ ☐ ☁ ☐ ⛅ ☐ 🌧 ☐ 🌧 ☐ 🌨 ☐ 🚩 _____ 🌡 _____

Firearm:	
Bullet:	Seating Depth:
Powder:	Grains:
Primer:	
Brass:	
Distance:	

Overall Results

☐ Poor   ☐ Fair   ☐ Good   ☐ Excellent

Notes

_____
_____
_____

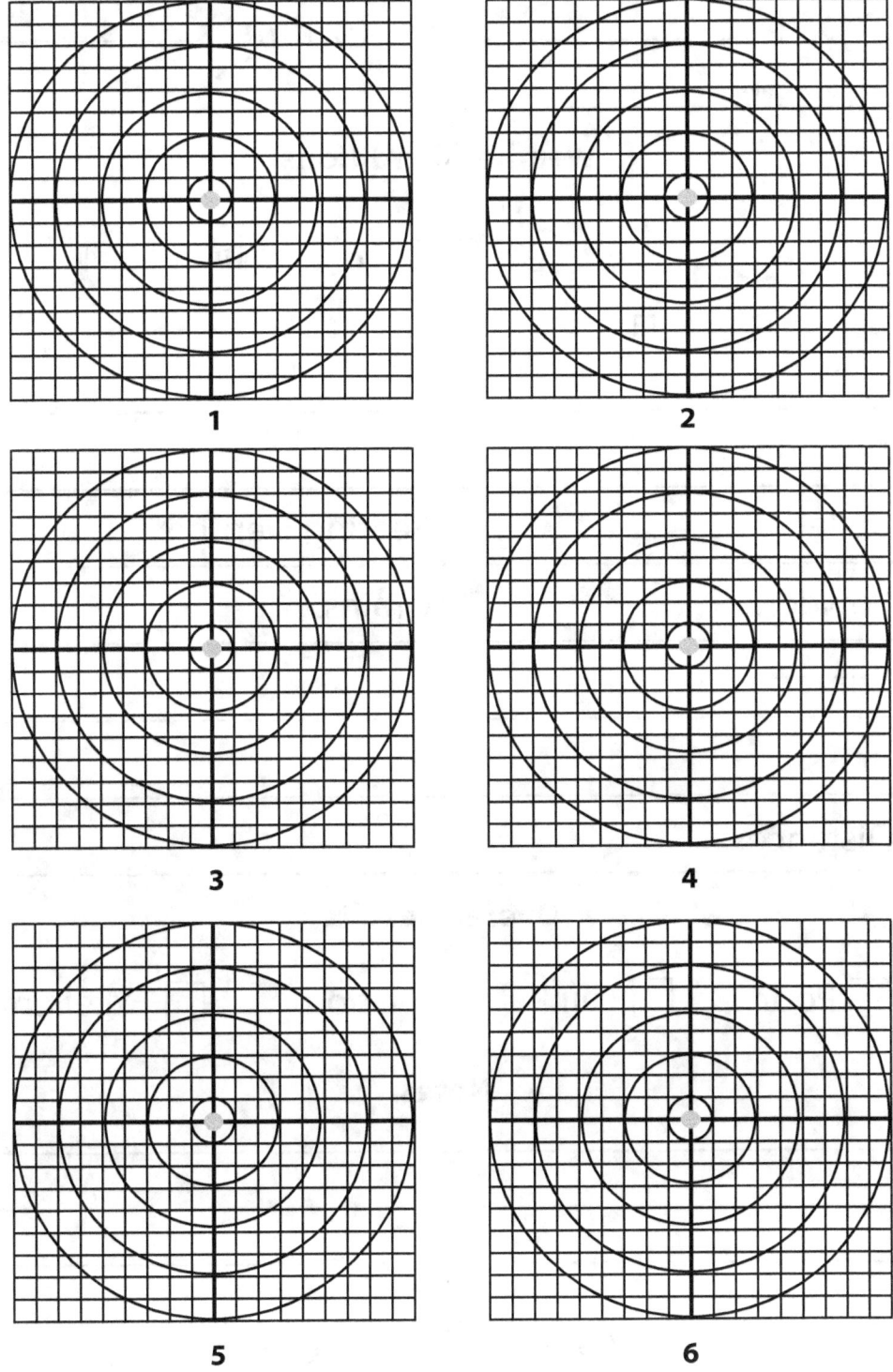

Date: _____ Time: _____

Location: _____

Weather Conditions

☀ ☁ ⛅ 🌦 🌧 🌨 🚩 🌡
☐ ☐ ☐ ☐ ☐ ☐ _____ _____

Firearm:	
Bullet:	Seating Depth:
Powder:	Grains:
Primer:	
Brass:	
Distance:	

Overall Results

☐ Poor   ☐ Fair   ☐ Good   ☐ Excellent

Notes

_____

_____

_____

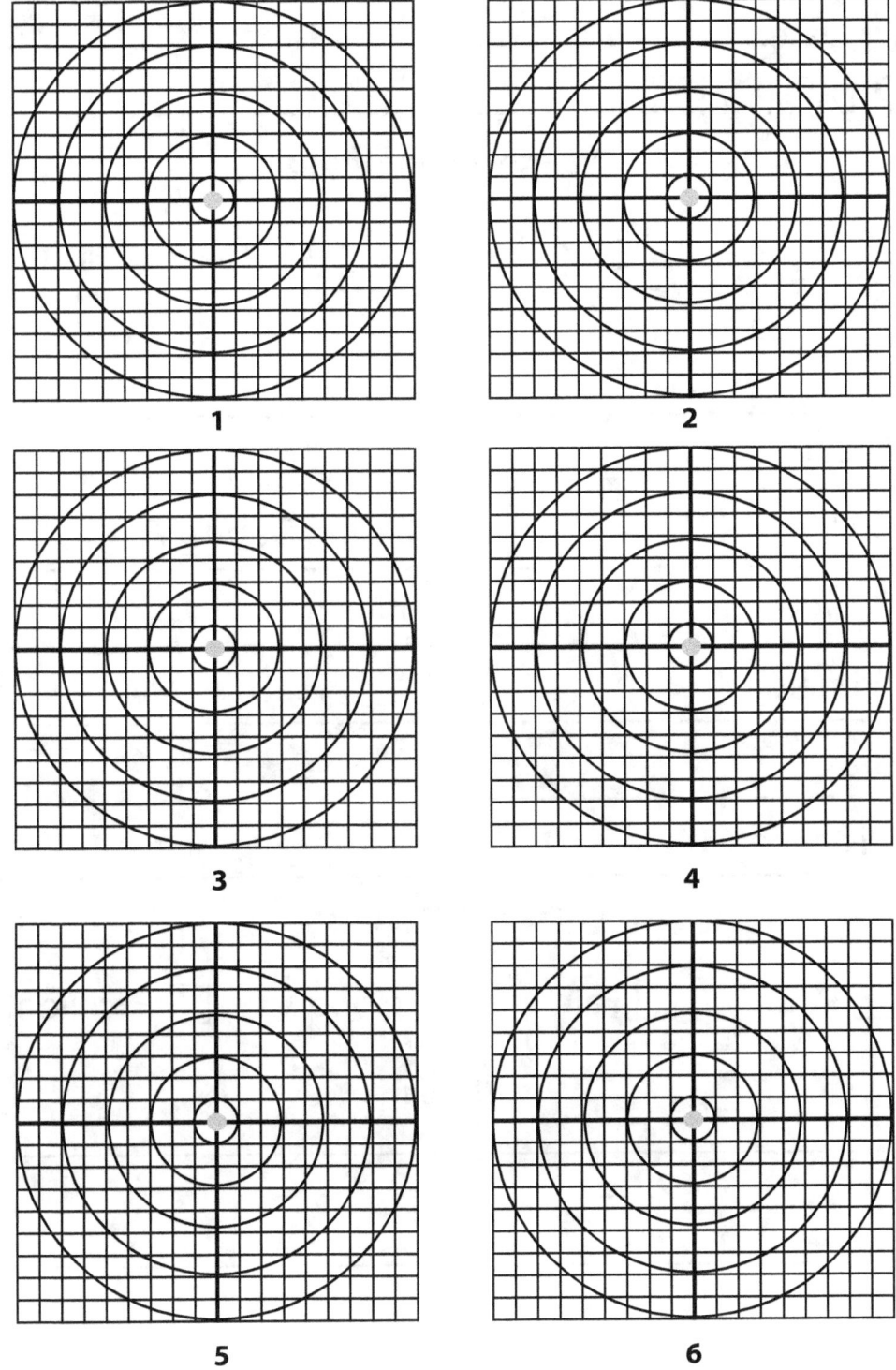

Date: _____ Time: _____

Location: _____

Weather Conditions

☀ ☁ ⛅ 🌦 🌧 🌨 🚩 🌡
☐ ☐ ☐ ☐ ☐ ☐ ____ ____

Firearm:	
Bullet:	Seating Depth:
Powder:	Grains:
Primer:	
Brass:	
Distance:	

Overall Results

☐ Poor   ☐ Fair   ☐ Good   ☐ Excellent

Notes

_____
_____
_____

☆ ☆ ☆ ☆ ☆

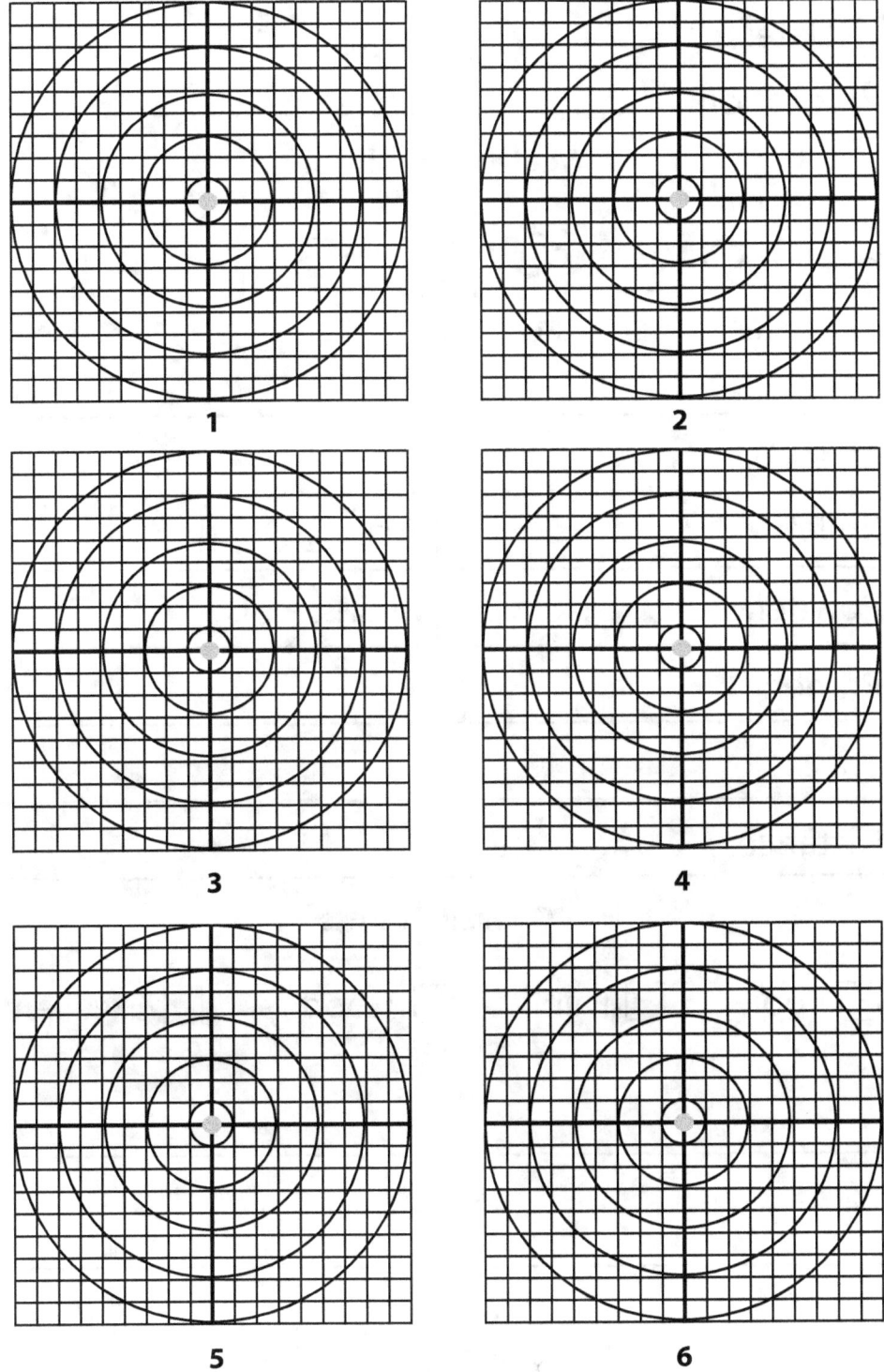

📅 Date: _____ 🕐 Time: _____

📍 Location: _____

Weather Conditions

☀️ ⛅ 🌥️ 🌧️ 🌧️ 🌨️ 🚩 🌡️
☐   ☐   ☐   ☐   ☐   ☐   ___ ___

Firearm:	
Bullet:	Seating Depth:
Powder:	Grains:
Primer:	
Brass:	
Distance:	

Overall Results

☐ Poor   ☐ Fair   ☐ Good   ☐ Excellent

Notes

_____
_____
_____

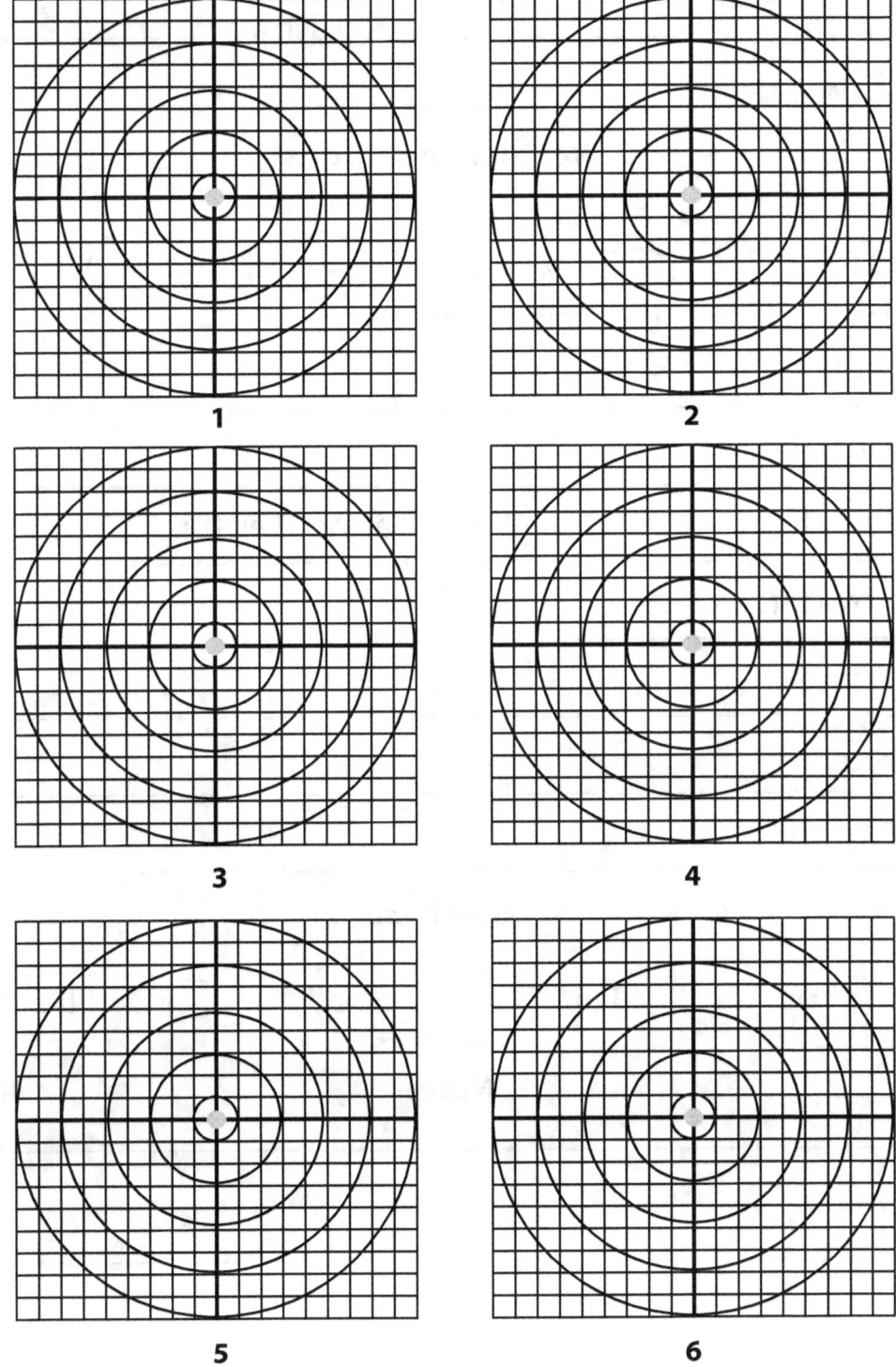

Date: _____ Time: _____
Location: _____

Weather Conditions

☀ ☁ ⛅ 🌦 🌧 🌨 🚩 🌡
☐ ☐ ☐ ☐ ☐ ☐ _____ _____

Firearm:	
Bullet:	Seating Depth:
Powder:	Grains:
Primer:	
Brass:	
Distance:	

Overall Results

☐ Poor   ☐ Fair   ☐ Good   ☐ Excellent

Notes

_____
_____
_____

☆ ☆ ☆ ☆ ☆

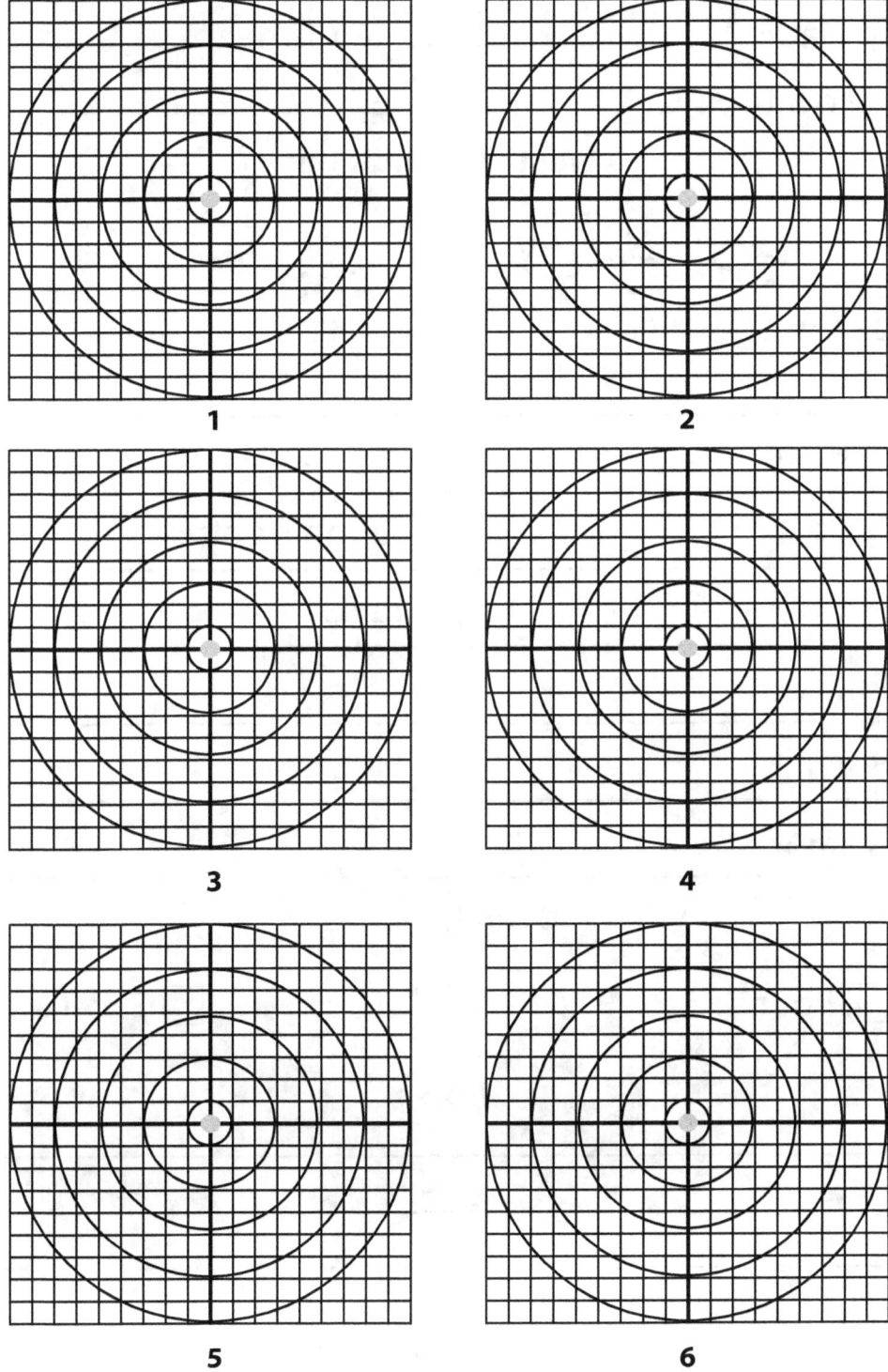

Date: _____ Time: _____

Location: _____

Weather Conditions

☀ ☁ ⛅ 🌥 🌧 🌨 🚩 🌡
☐ ☐ ☐ ☐ ☐ ☐ _____ _____

Firearm:	
Bullet:	Seating Depth:
Powder:	Grains:
Primer:	
Brass:	
Distance:	

Overall Results

☐ Poor ☐ Fair ☐ Good ☐ Excellent

Notes

_____
_____
_____

☆ ☆ ☆ ☆ ☆

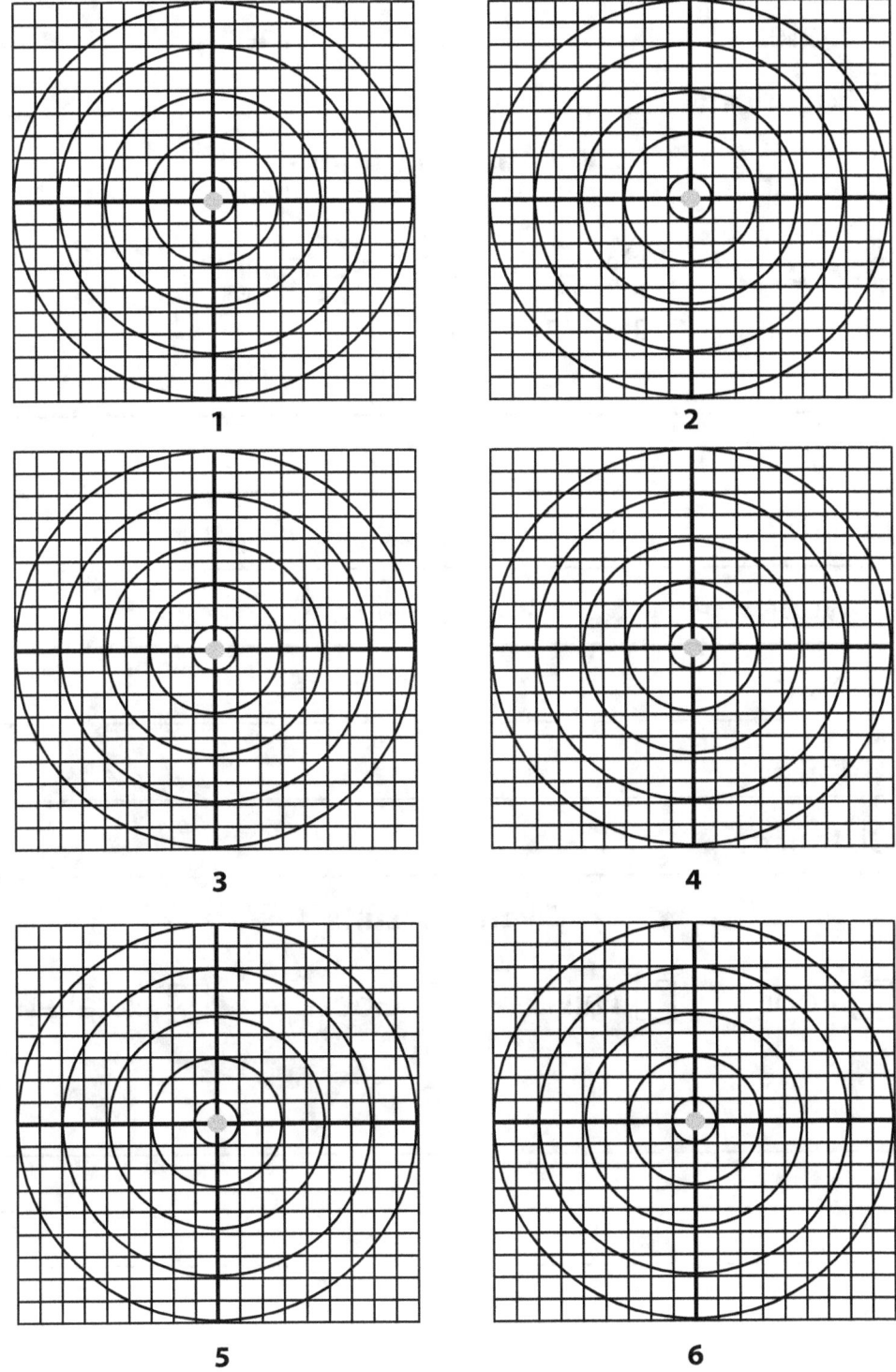

📅 Date: _____   🕐 Time: _____

📍 Location: _____

Weather Conditions

☀️ ☁️ ⛅ ☁️ 🌧️ 🌨️ 🚩 🌡️
☐   ☐   ☐   ☐   ☐   ☐   ___ ___

Firearm:	
Bullet:	Seating Depth:
Powder:	Grains:
Primer:	
Brass:	
Distance:	

Overall Results

☐ Poor   ☐ Fair   ☐ Good   ☐ Excellent

Notes

_____
_____
_____

☆ ☆ ☆ ☆ ☆

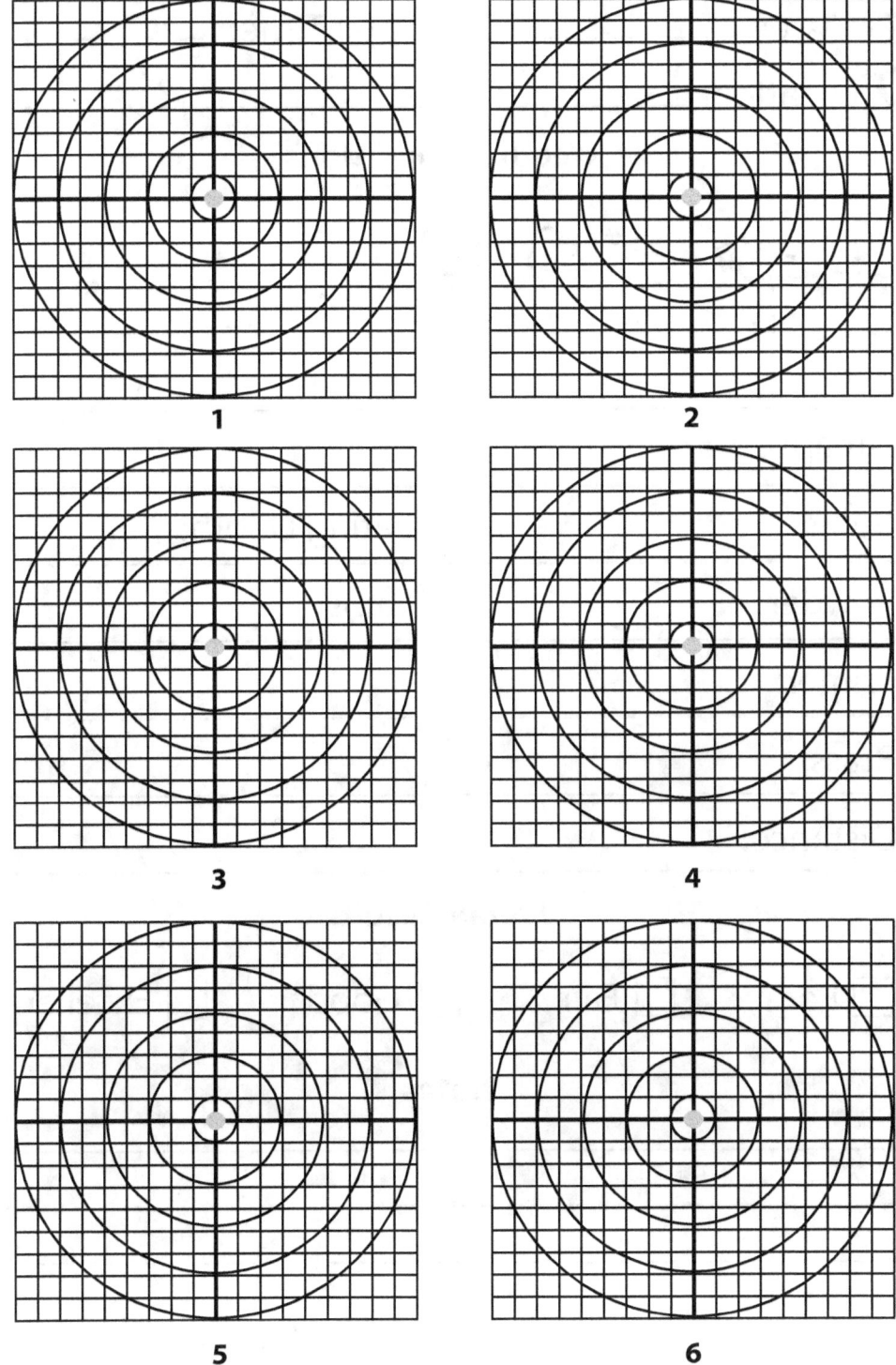

Date: _____ Time: _____

Location: _____

Weather Conditions

☀ ☁ ⛅ 🌦 🌧 🌨 🚩 🌡
☐ ☐ ☐ ☐ ☐ ☐ _____ _____

Firearm:	
Bullet:	Seating Depth:
Powder:	Grains:
Primer:	
Brass:	
Distance:	

Overall Results

☐ Poor   ☐ Fair   ☐ Good   ☐ Excellent

Notes

_____
_____
_____

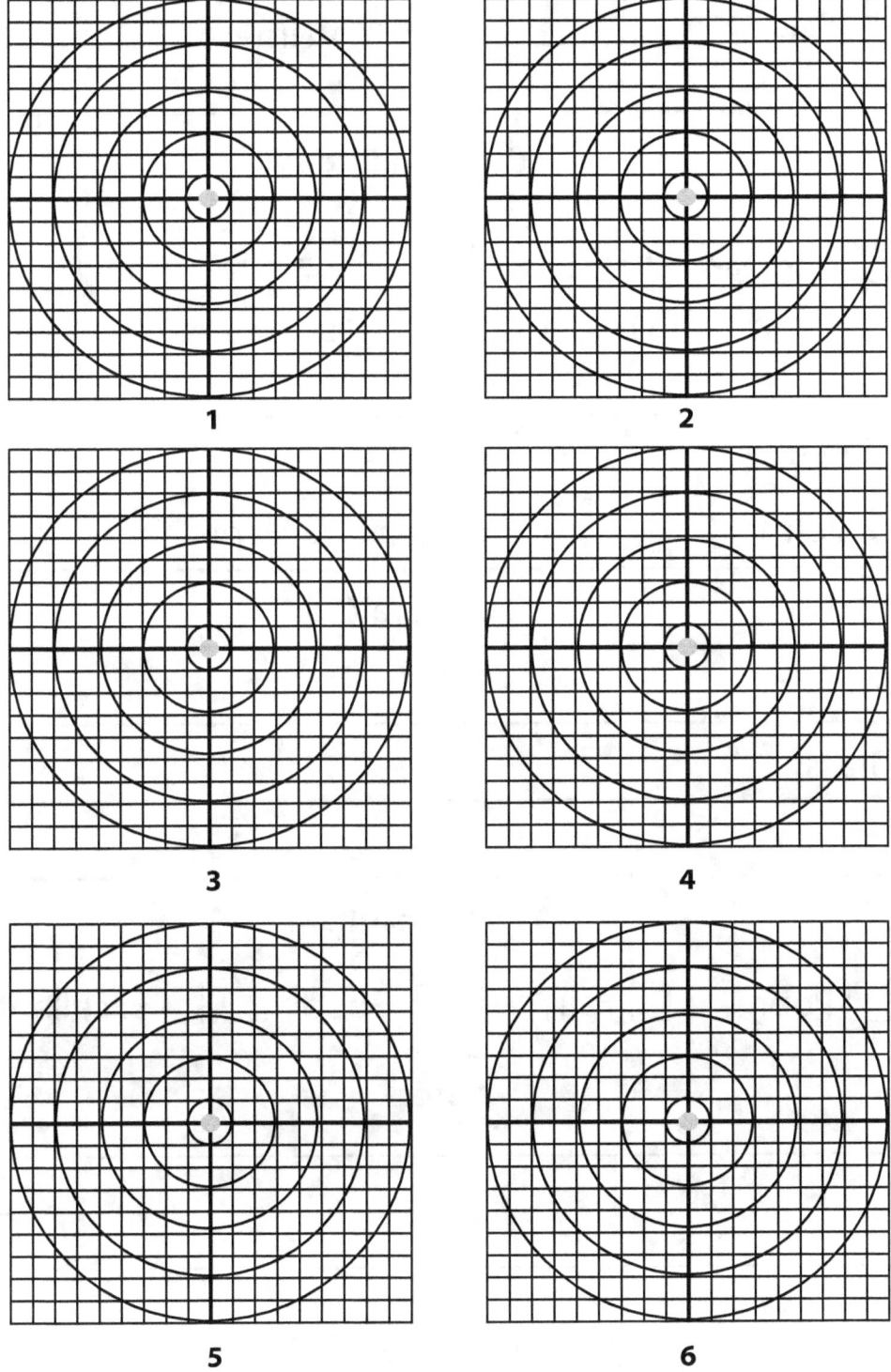

Date: _____ Time: _____

Location: _____

Weather Conditions

☀ ☁ ⛅ 🌦 🌧 🌨 🚩 🌡
☐ ☐ ☐ ☐ ☐ ☐ _____ _____

Firearm:	
Bullet:	Seating Depth:
Powder:	Grains:
Primer:	
Brass:	
Distance:	

Overall Results

☐ Poor ☐ Fair ☐ Good ☐ Excellent

Notes

_____
_____
_____

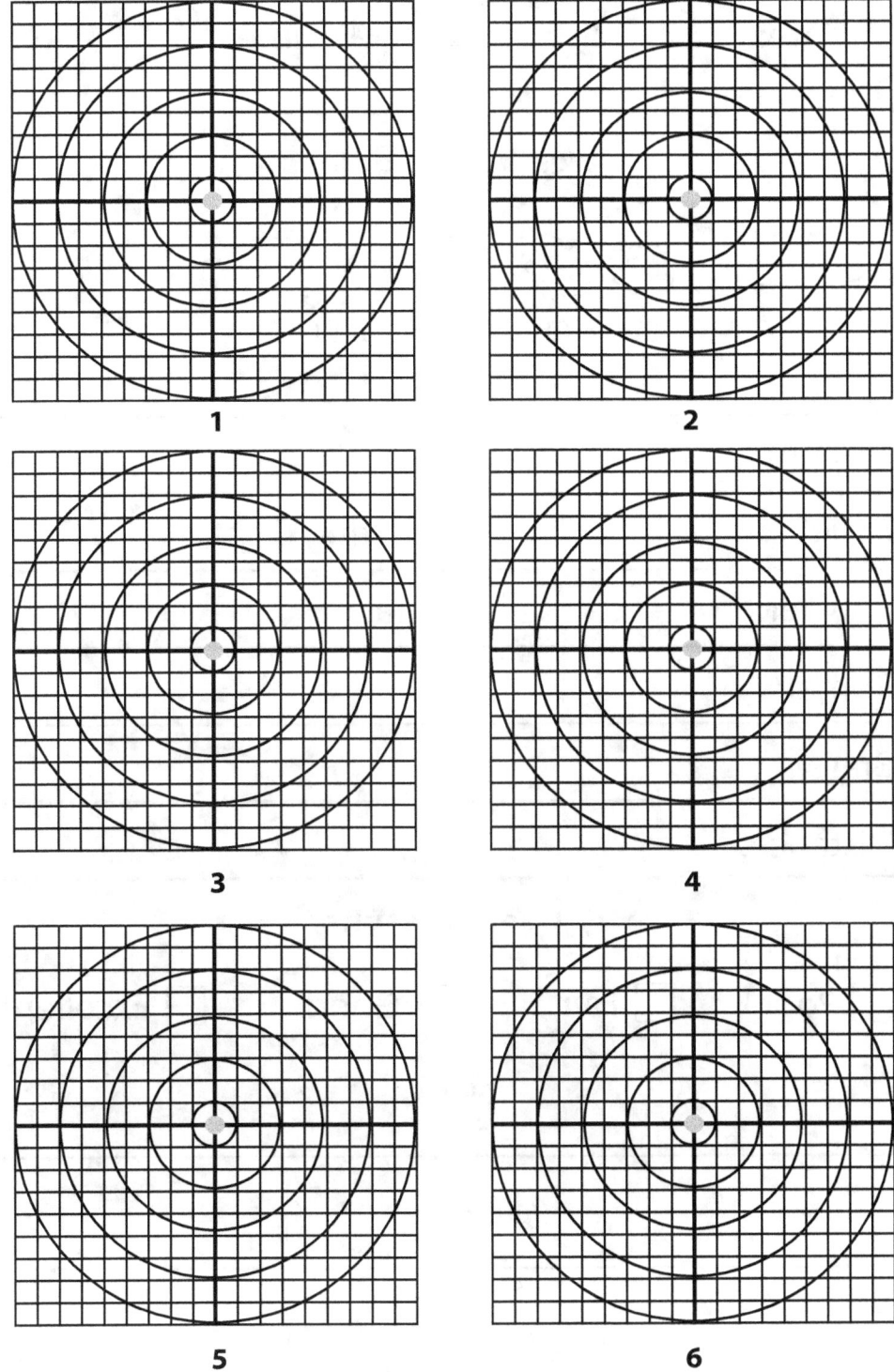

📅 Date: _____ 🕐 Time: _____

📍 Location: _____

Weather Conditions

☀ ⛅ 🌤 🌧 🌧 🌨 ⚑ 🌡
☐ ☐ ☐ ☐ ☐ ☐ _____ _____

Firearm:	
Bullet:	Seating Depth:
Powder:	Grains:
Primer:	
Brass:	
Distance:	

Overall Results

☐ Poor ☐ Fair ☐ Good ☐ Excellent

Notes

_____
_____

☆ ☆ ☆ ☆ ☆

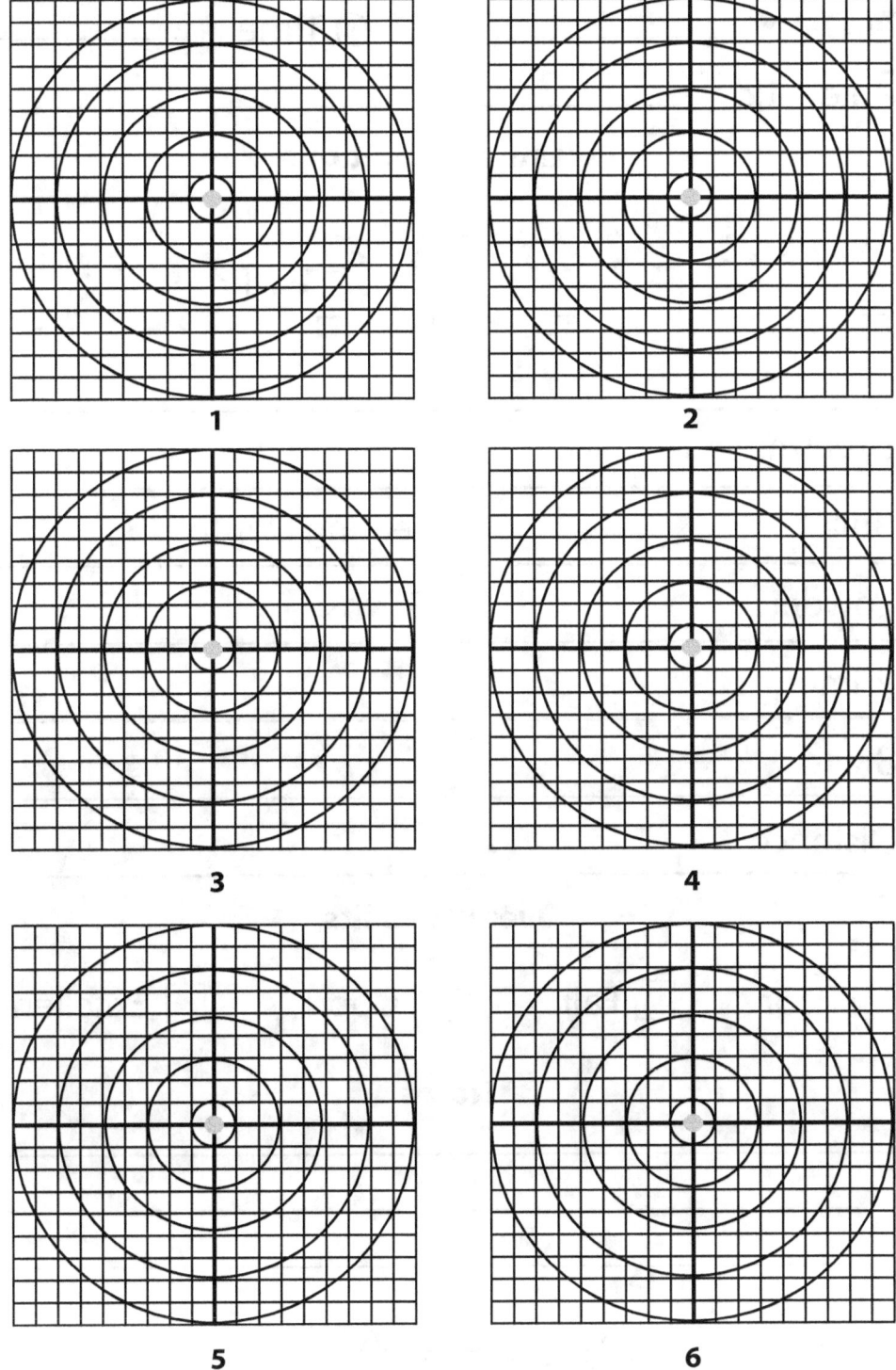

Date: _____   Time: _____
Location: _____

Weather Conditions

☀ ☁ ⛅ 🌦 🌧 🌨 🚩 🌡
☐   ☐   ☐   ☐   ☐   ☐   ____   ____

Firearm:	
Bullet:	Seating Depth:
Powder:	Grains:
Primer:	
Brass:	
Distance:	

Overall Results

☐ Poor   ☐ Fair   ☐ Good   ☐ Excellent

Notes

_____
_____
_____

☆ ☆ ☆ ☆ ☆

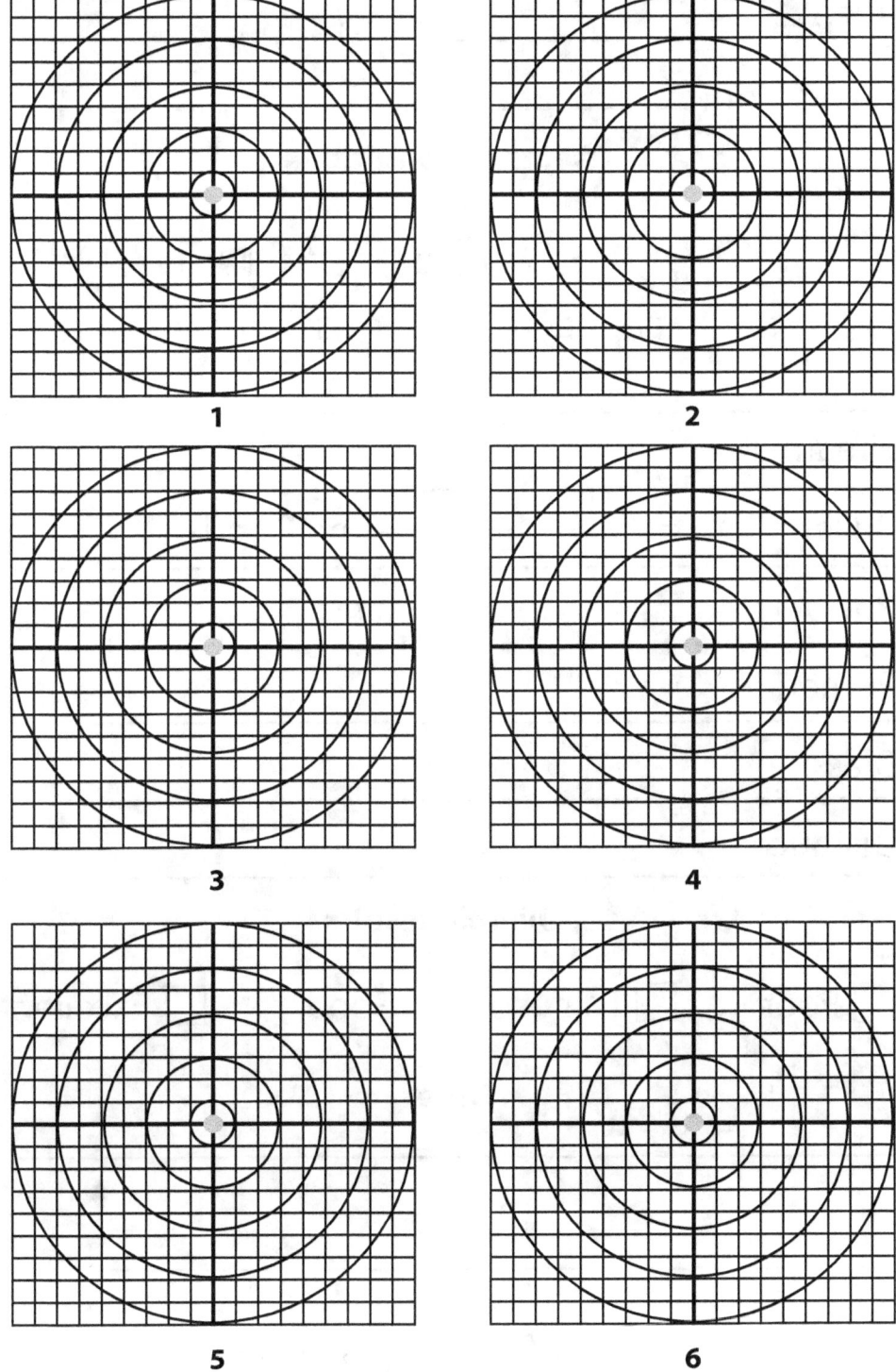

Date: _____   Time: _____

Location: _____

Weather Conditions

☀ ☐   ☁ ☐   ⛅ ☐   🌧 ☐   🌧 ☐   🌨 ☐   🚩 _____   🌡 _____

Firearm:	
Bullet:	Seating Depth:
Powder:	Grains:
Primer:	
Brass:	
Distance:	

Overall Results

☐ Poor   ☐ Fair   ☐ Good   ☐ Excellent

Notes

_____
_____
_____

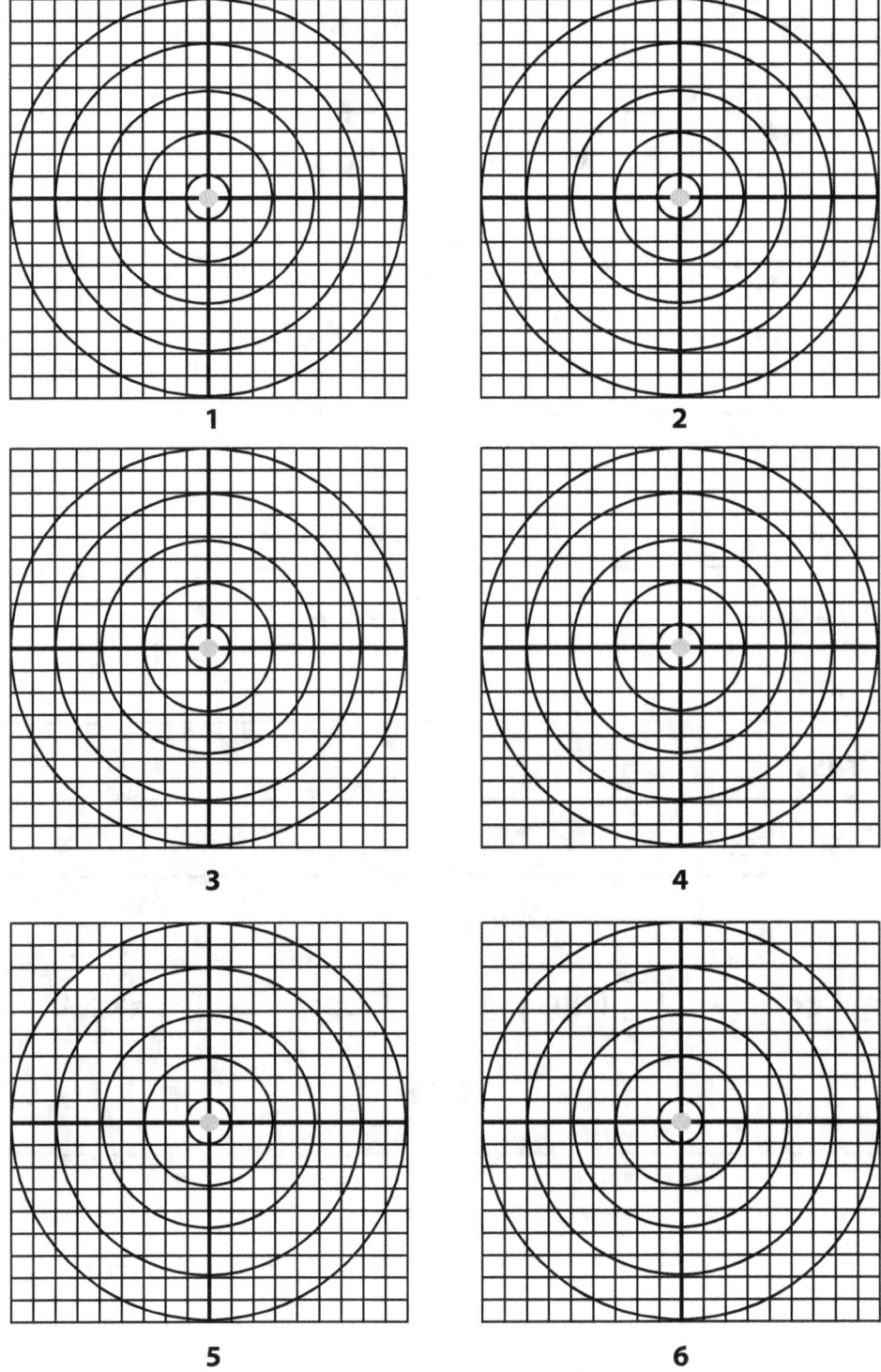

Date: _____ Time: _____
Location: _____

Weather Conditions

☀ ☁ ⛅ 🌧 🌨 🌧 ⚑ 🌡
☐   ☐   ☐   ☐   ☐   ☐   ____   ____

Firearm:	
Bullet:	Seating Depth:
Powder:	Grains:
Primer:	
Brass:	
Distance:	

Overall Results

☐ Poor   ☐ Fair   ☐ Good   ☐ Excellent

Notes

_____
_____
_____

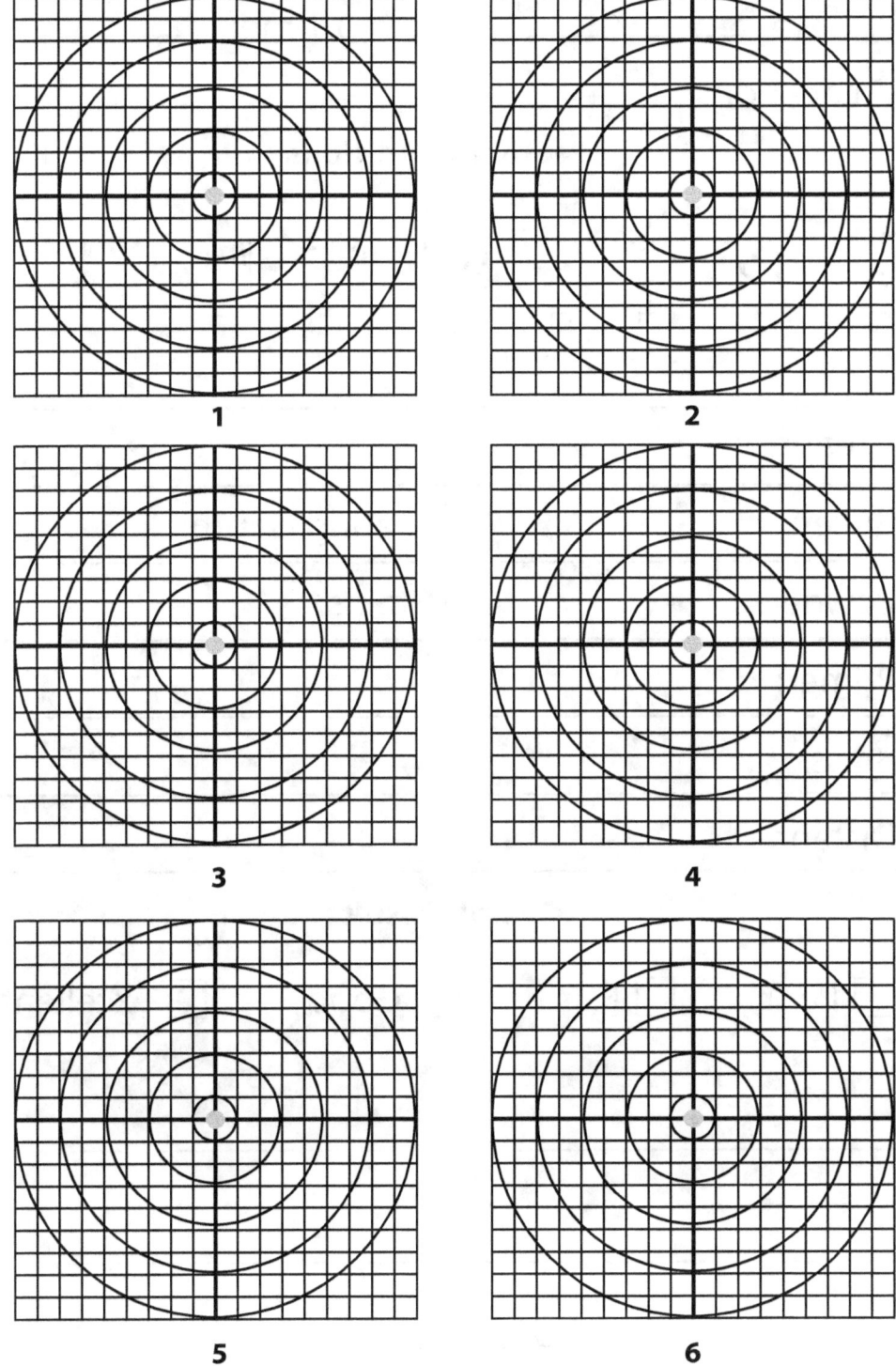

📅 Date: _____ 🕐 Time: _____

📍 Location: _____

Weather Conditions

☀ ☁ ⛅ 🌧 🌨 🌩 🚩 🌡
☐   ☐   ☐   ☐   ☐   ☐   _____ _____

Firearm:	
Bullet:	Seating Depth:
Powder:	Grains:
Primer:	
Brass:	
Distance:	

Overall Results

☐ Poor ☐ Fair ☐ Good ☐ Excellent

Notes

_____

_____

☆ ☆ ☆ ☆ ☆

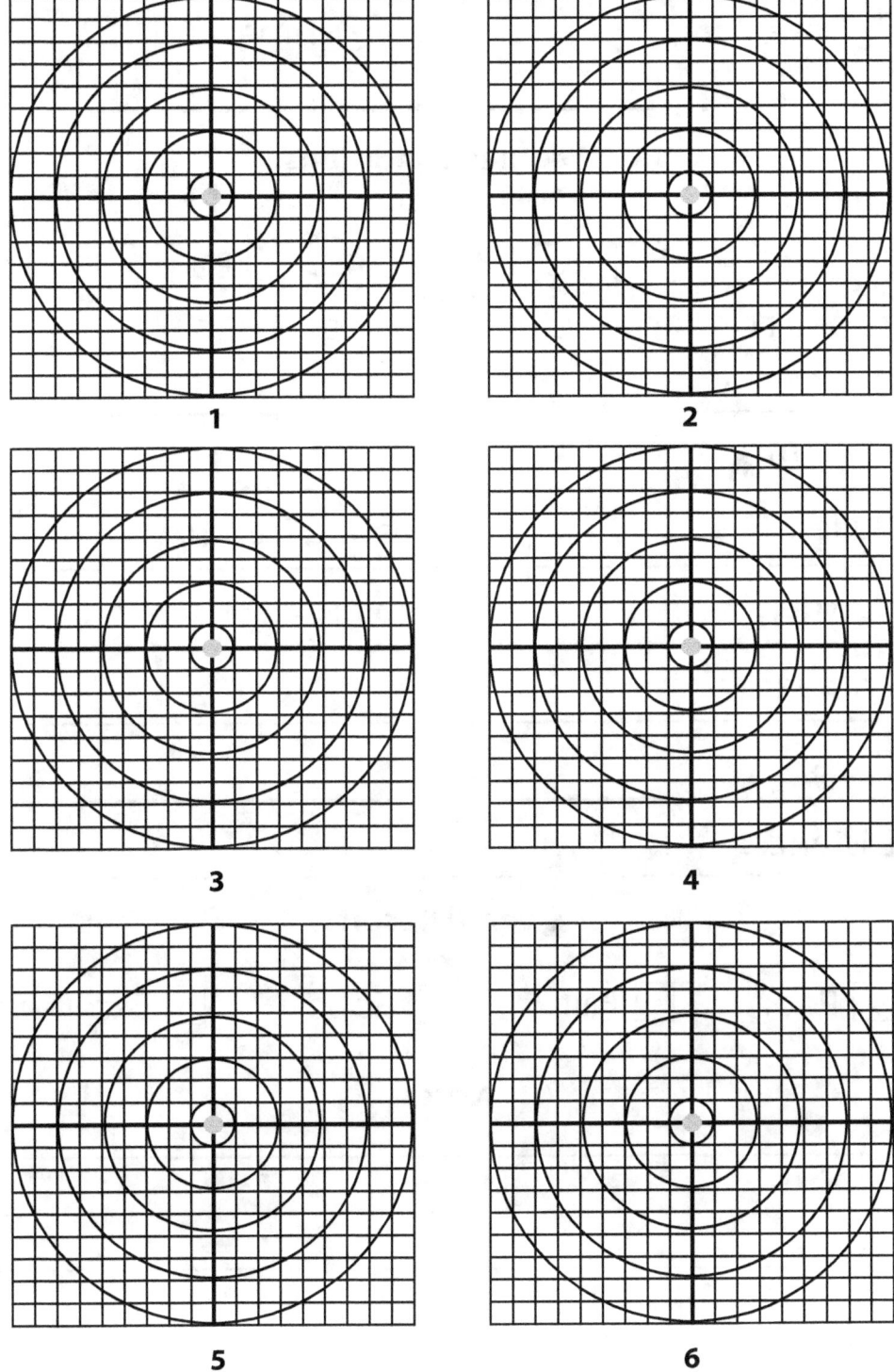

Date: _____ ⏱ Time: _____

 Location: _____

Weather Conditions

☐   ☐   ☐   ☐   ☐   ☐   ⚑ _____   🌡 _____

Firearm:	
Bullet:	Seating Depth:
Powder:	Grains:
Primer:	
Brass:	
Distance:	

Overall Results

☐ Poor   ☐ Fair   ☐ Good   ☐ Excellent

Notes

_____

_____

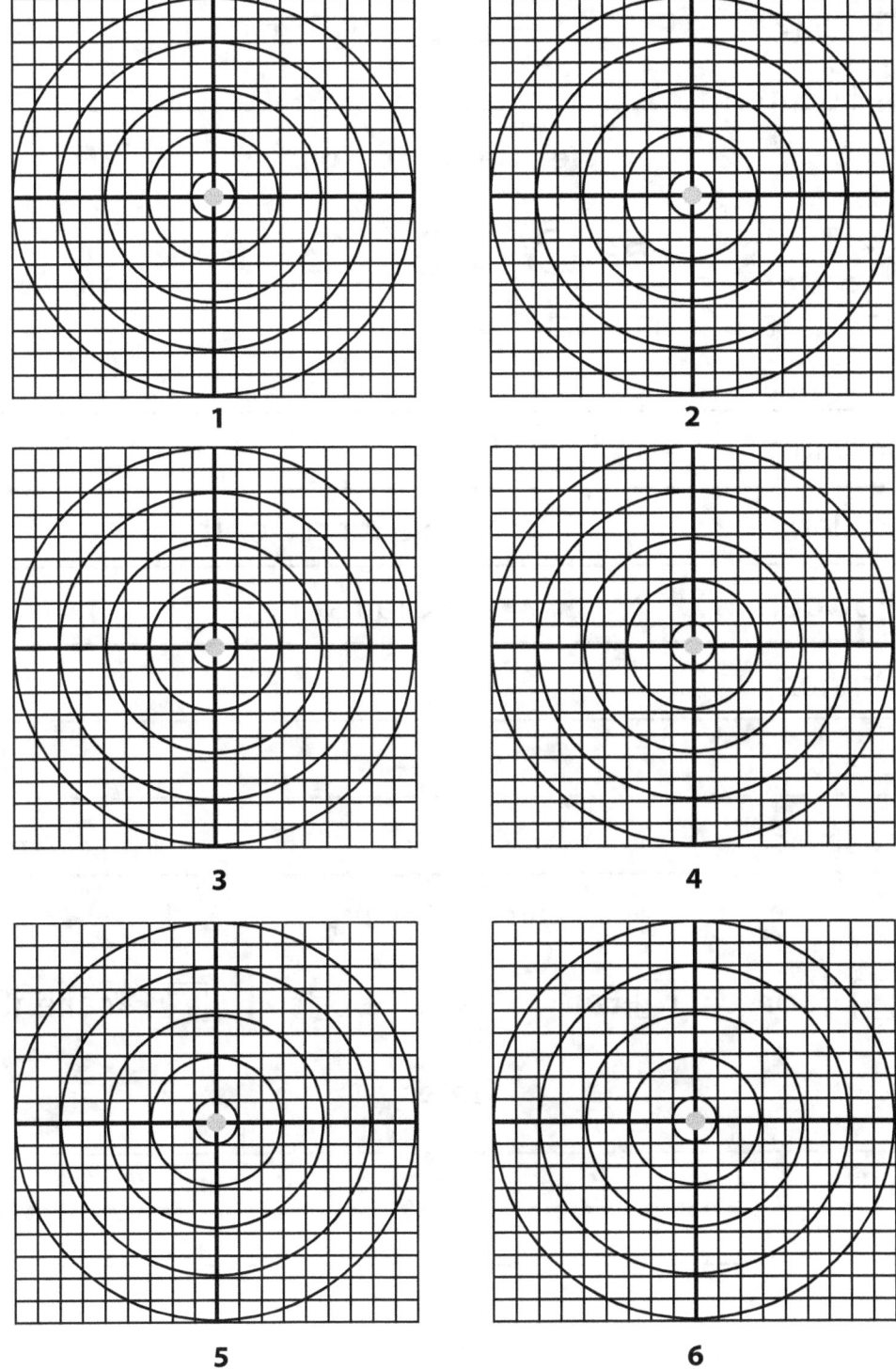

Date: _____   Time: _____

Location: _____

Weather Conditions

☀ ☐ ⛅ ☐ 🌤 ☐ 🌧 ☐ 🌧 ☐ 🌨 ☐ 🚩 _____ 🌡 _____

Firearm:	
Bullet:	Seating Depth:
Powder:	Grains:
Primer:	
Brass:	
Distance:	

Overall Results

☐ Poor   ☐ Fair   ☐ Good   ☐ Excellent

Notes

_____

_____

_____

☆ ☆ ☆ ☆ ☆

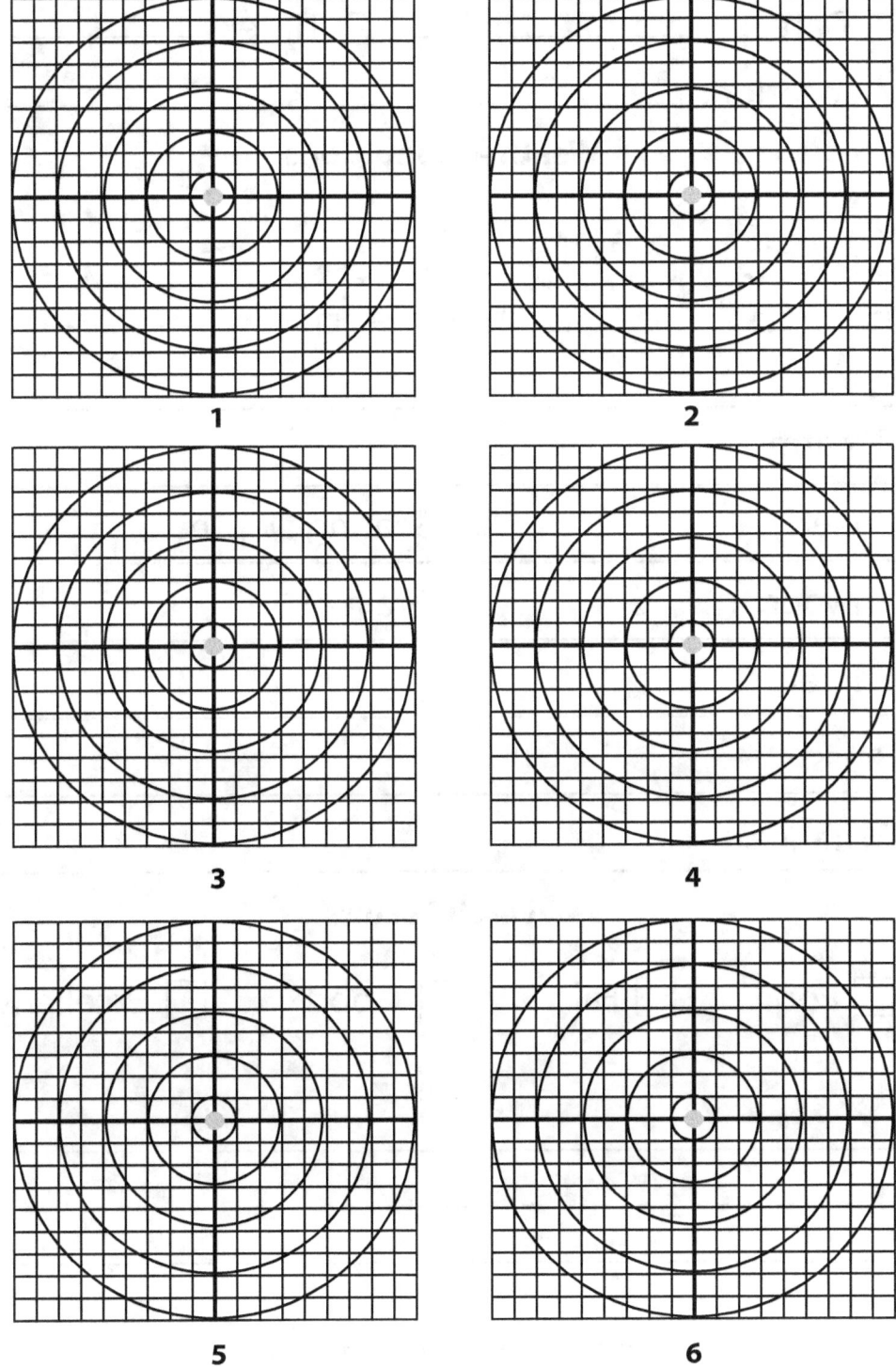

Date: _____ Time: _____

Location: _____

Weather Conditions

☀ ☁ ⛅ 🌦 🌧 🌨 ⚑ 🌡
☐ ☐ ☐ ☐ ☐ ☐

Firearm:	
Bullet:	Seating Depth:
Powder:	Grains:
Primer:	
Brass:	
Distance:	

Overall Results

☐ Poor   ☐ Fair   ☐ Good   ☐ Excellent

Notes

_____

_____

_____

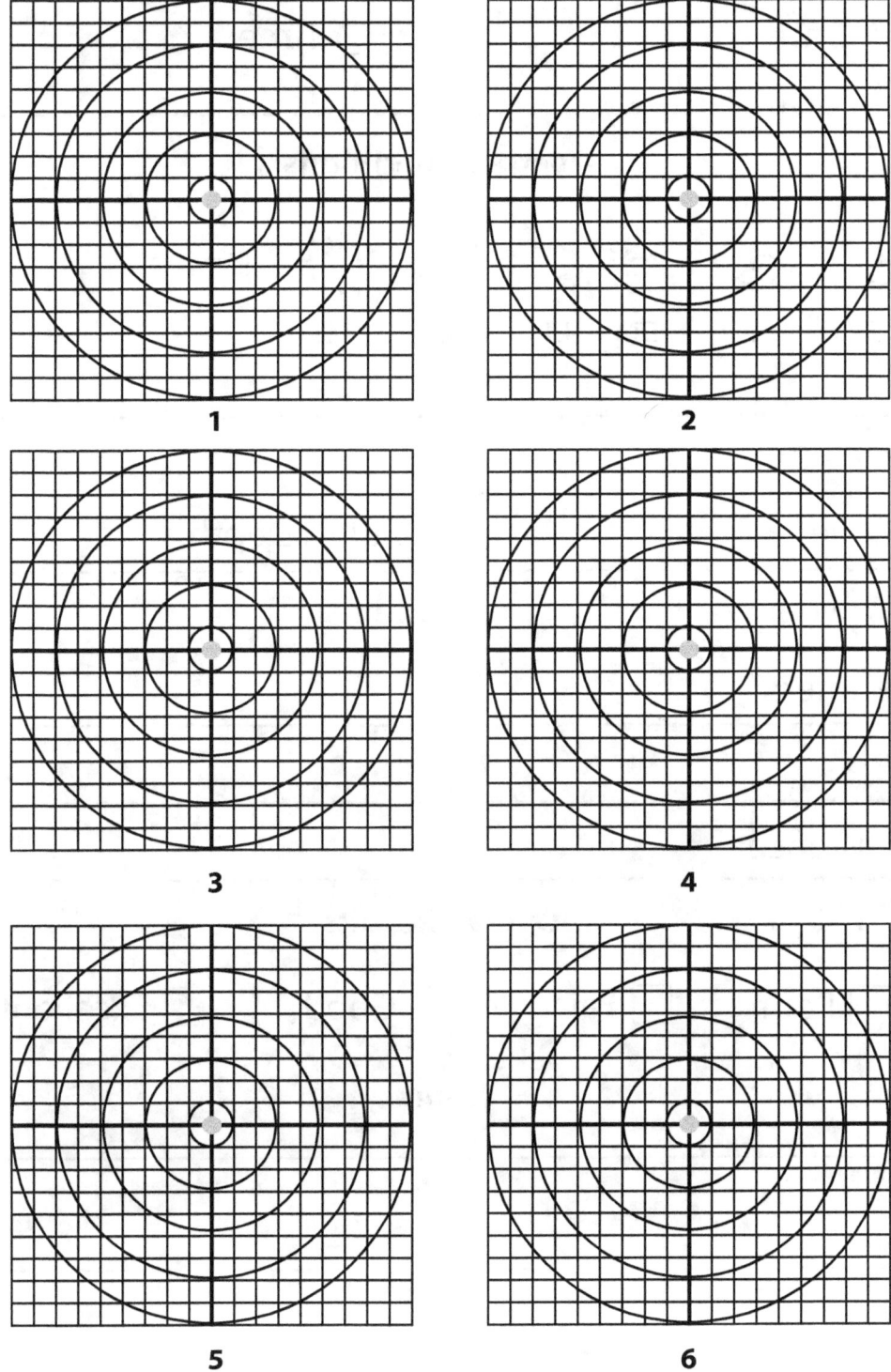

Date: _____ Time: _____
Location: _____

Weather Conditions

☀ ☁ ⛅ 🌦 🌧 🌨 🚩 🌡
☐ ☐ ☐ ☐ ☐ ☐ ____ ____

Firearm:	
Bullet:	Seating Depth:
Powder:	Grains:
Primer:	
Brass:	
Distance:	

Overall Results

☐ Poor   ☐ Fair   ☐ Good   ☐ Excellent

Notes

_____
_____
_____

☆ ☆ ☆ ☆ ☆

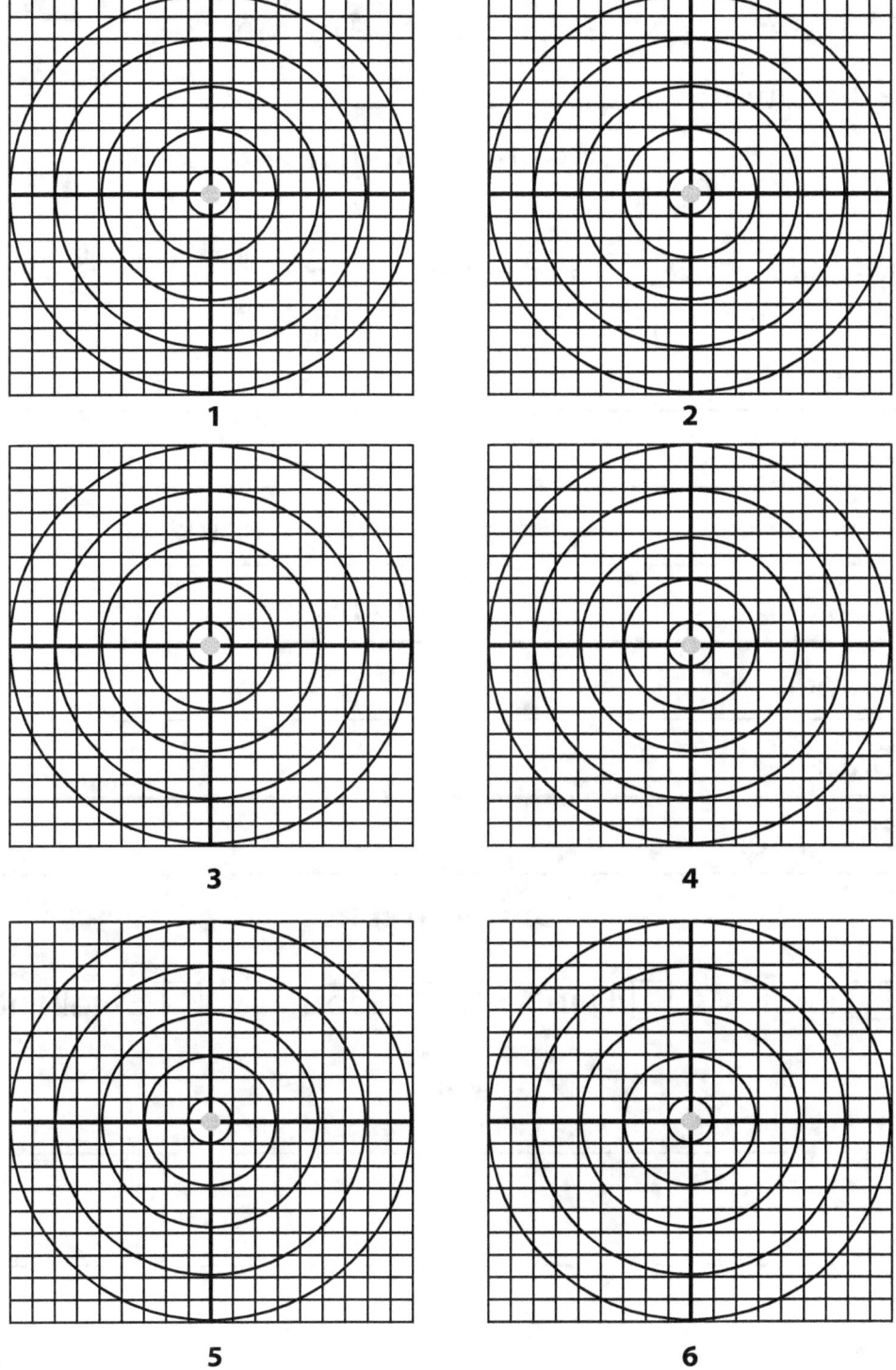

Date: _____ Time: _____
Location: _____

Weather Conditions

☀️ ☁️ 🌤️ 🌧️ 🌧️ 🌨️ 🚩 🌡️
☐ ☐ ☐ ☐ ☐ ☐

Firearm:	
Bullet:	Seating Depth:
Powder:	Grains:
Primer:	
Brass:	
Distance:	

Overall Results

☐ Poor   ☐ Fair   ☐ Good   ☐ Excellent

Notes

_____
_____
_____

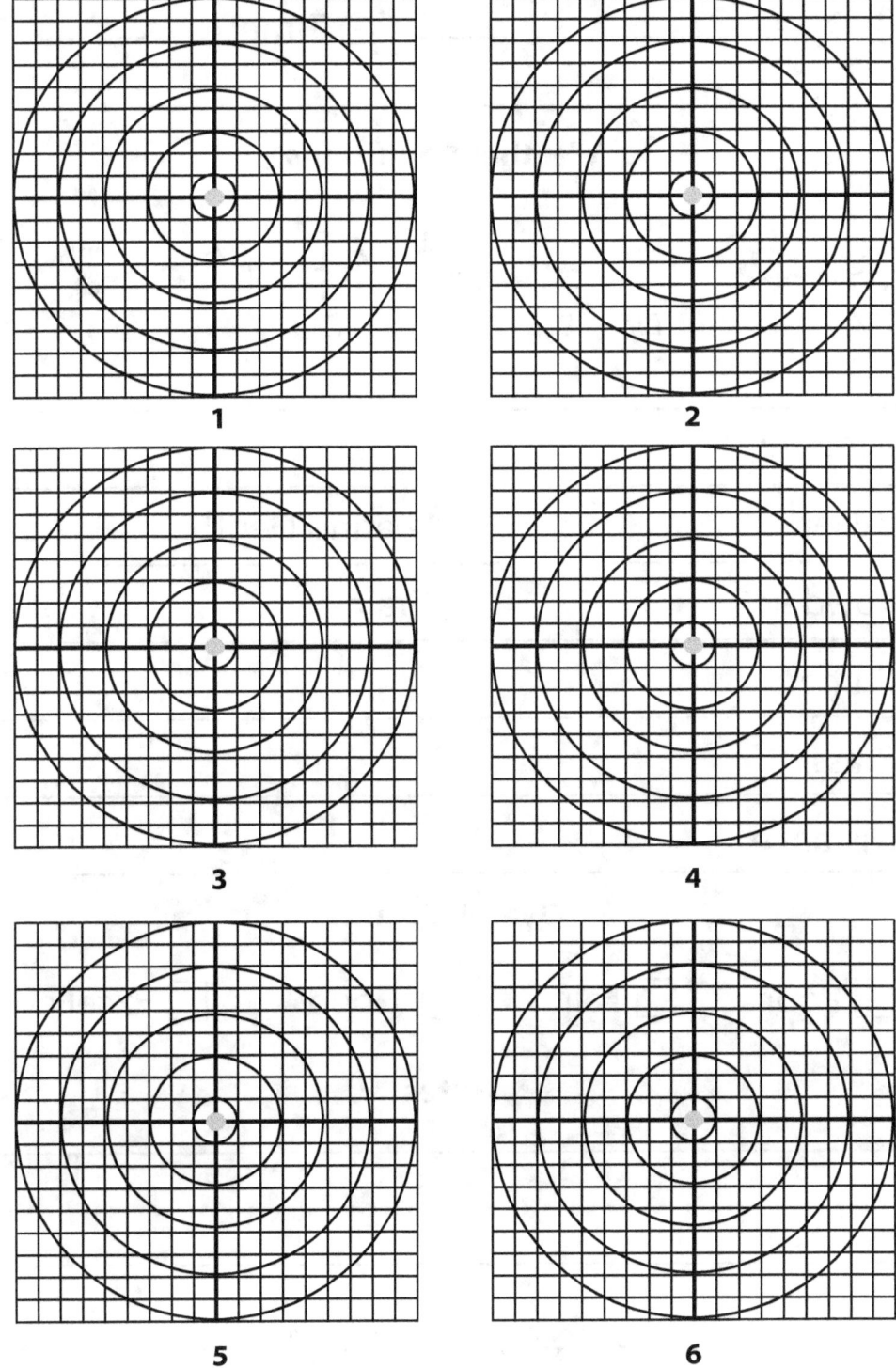

Date: _____ Time: _____

Location: _____

Weather Conditions

☀ ☁ ⛅ 🌦 🌧 🌨 🚩 🌡
☐ ☐ ☐ ☐ ☐ ☐

Firearm:	
Bullet:	Seating Depth:
Powder:	Grains:
Primer:	
Brass:	
Distance:	

Overall Results

☐ Poor   ☐ Fair   ☐ Good   ☐ Excellent

Notes

_____
_____
_____

☆ ☆ ☆ ☆ ☆

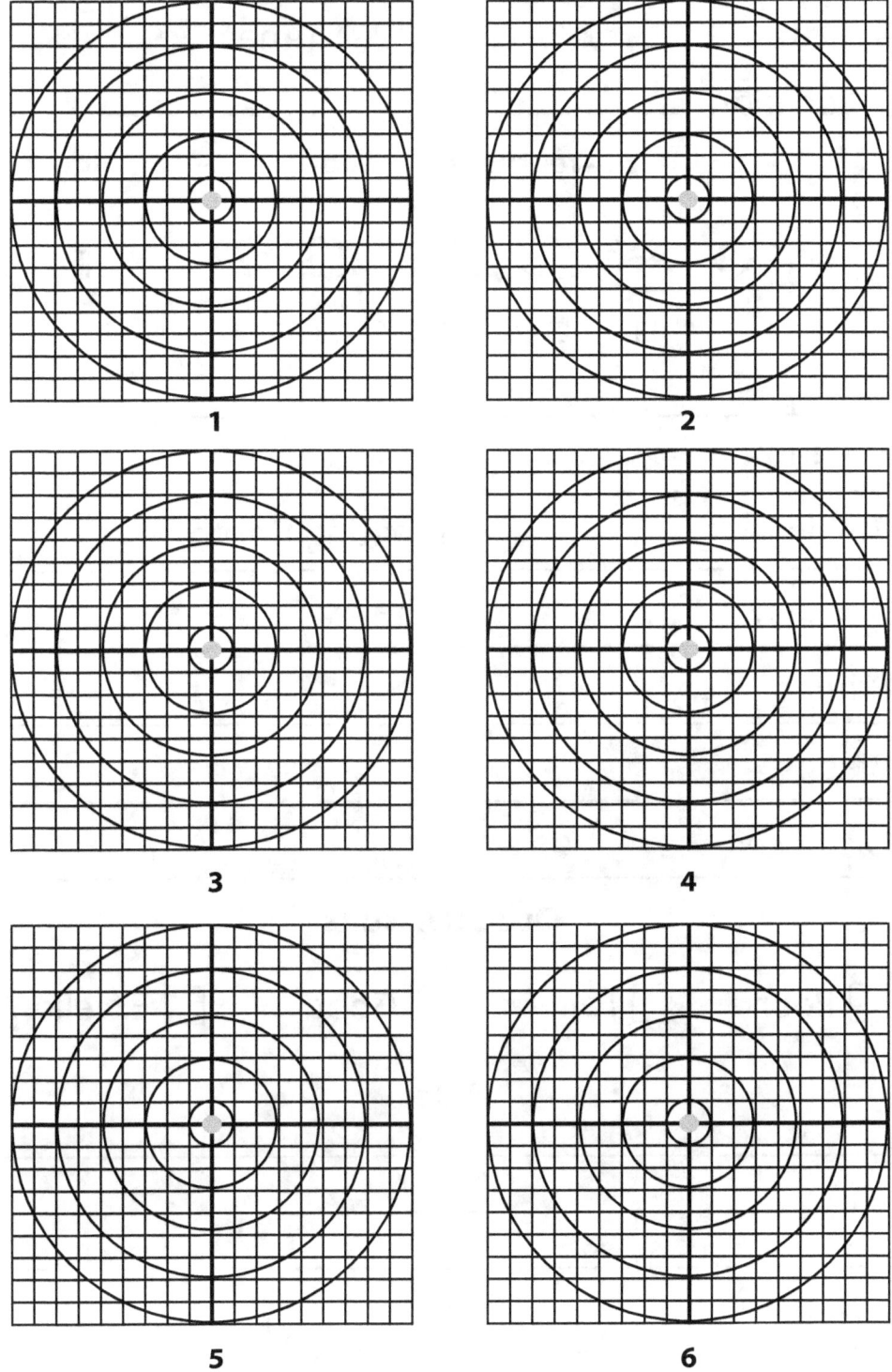

Date: _____ Time: _____

Location: _____

Weather Conditions

☀ ☁ ⛅ 🌦 🌧 🌨 🚩 🌡
☐ ☐ ☐ ☐ ☐ ☐ _____ _____

Firearm:	
Bullet:	Seating Depth:
Powder:	Grains:
Primer:	
Brass:	
Distance:	

Overall Results

☐ Poor   ☐ Fair   ☐ Good   ☐ Excellent

Notes

_____
_____
_____

☆ ☆ ☆ ☆ ☆

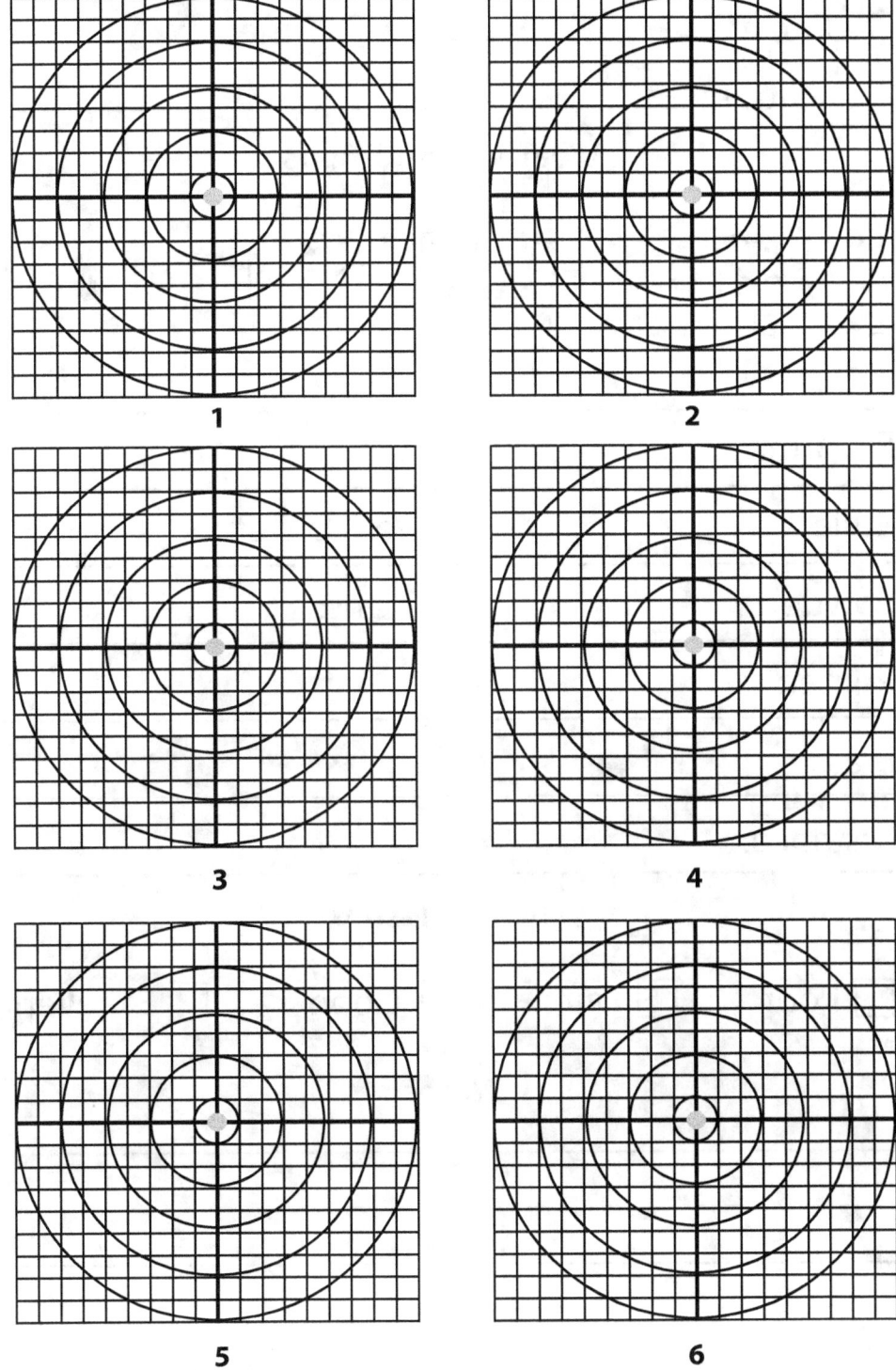

Date: _____ Time: _____

 Location: _____

Weather Conditions

☀ ☁ ⛅ 🌥 🌧 🌨 🚩 🌡
☐ ☐ ☐ ☐ ☐ ☐ ___ ___

Firearm:	
Bullet:	Seating Depth:
Powder:	Grains:
Primer:	
Brass:	
Distance:	

Overall Results

☐ Poor ☐ Fair ☐ Good ☐ Excellent

Notes

_____
_____
_____

☆ ☆ ☆ ☆ ☆

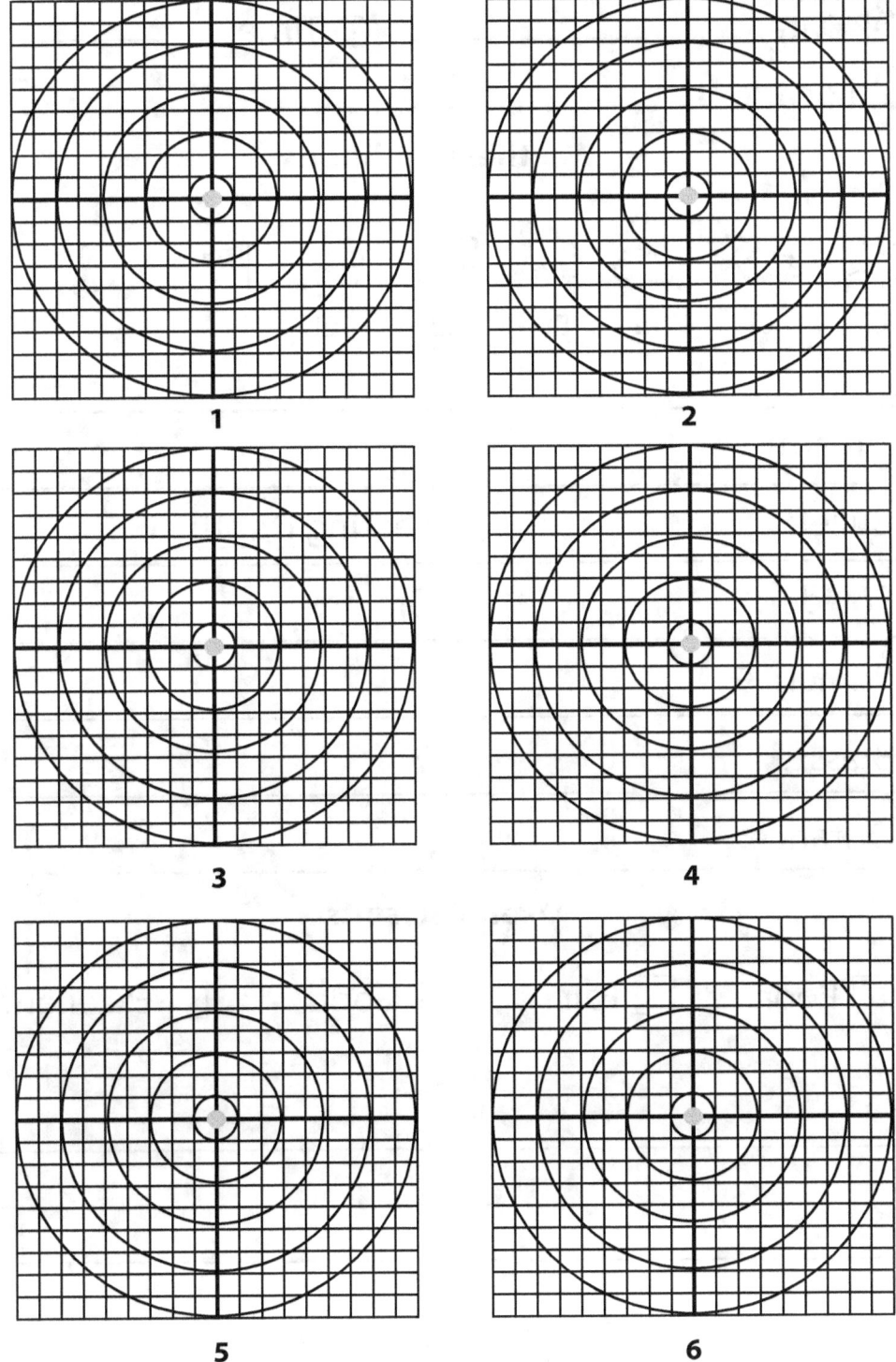

Date: _____ Time: _____

Location: _____

Weather Conditions

☀ ☁ ⛅ 🌦 🌧 🌨 🚩 🌡
☐ ☐ ☐ ☐ ☐ ☐

Firearm:	
Bullet:	Seating Depth:
Powder:	Grains:
Primer:	
Brass:	
Distance:	

Overall Results

☐ Poor ☐ Fair ☐ Good ☐ Excellent

Notes

_____
_____
_____

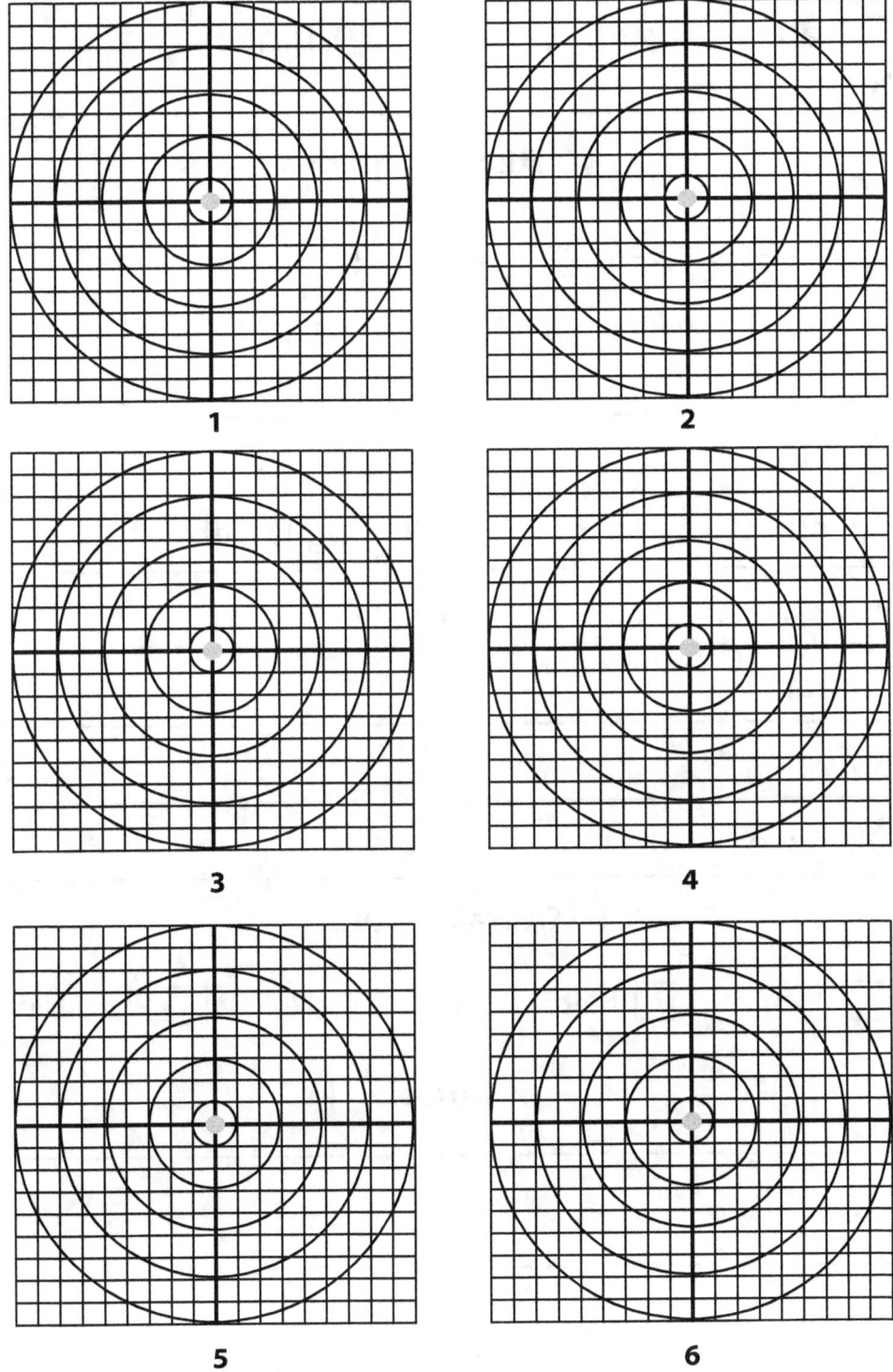

Date: _____   Time: _____

Location: _____

Weather Conditions

☀ ☁ ⛅ 🌧 🌧 🌨 🚩_____ 🌡_____
☐ ☐ ☐ ☐ ☐ ☐

Firearm:	
Bullet:	Seating Depth:
Powder:	Grains:
Primer:	
Brass:	
Distance:	

Overall Results

☐ Poor   ☐ Fair   ☐ Good   ☐ Excellent

Notes

_____
_____
_____

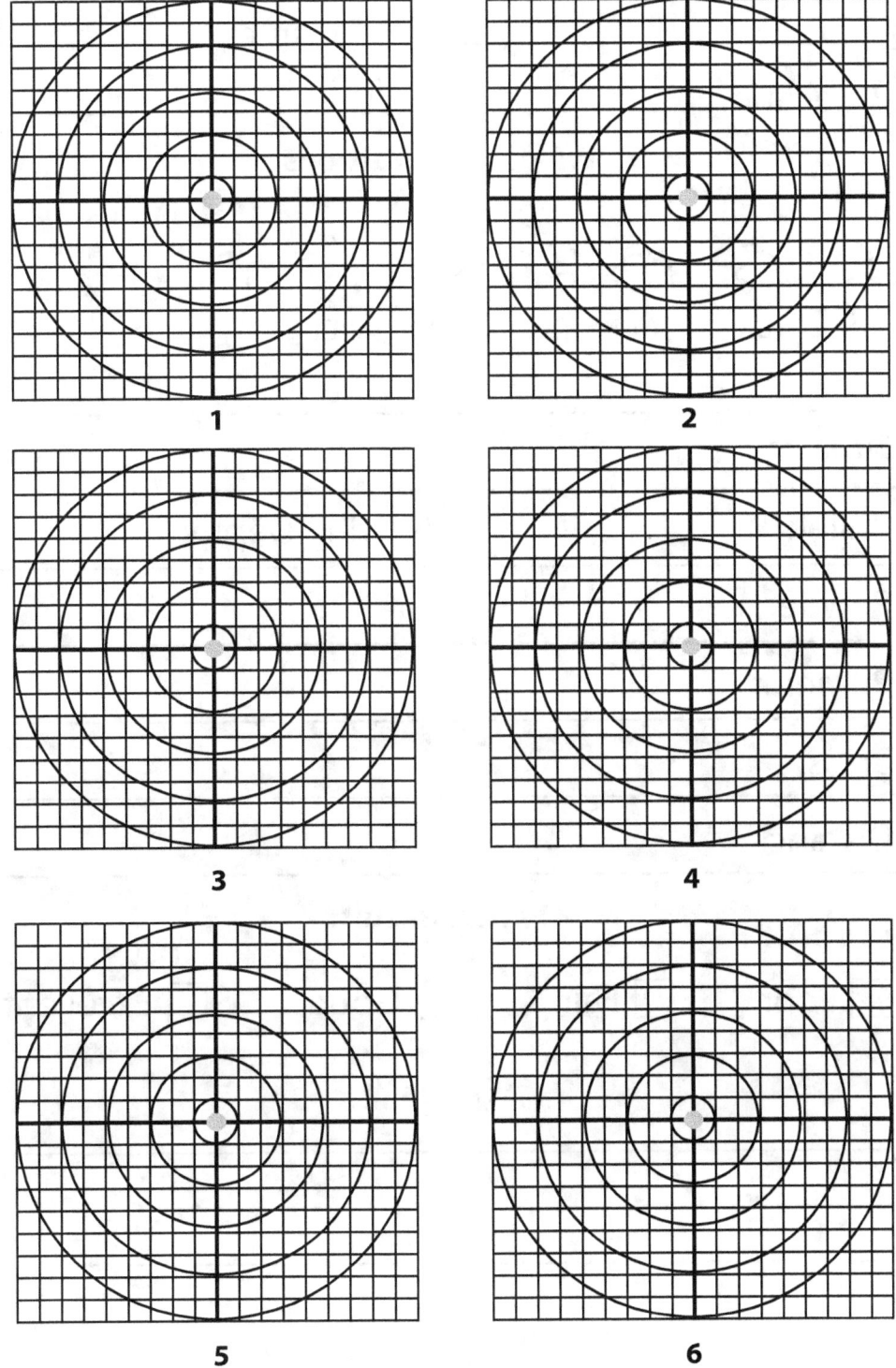

Date: _____ Time: _____

Location: _____

Weather Conditions

☀ ☁ ⛅ 🌦 🌧 🌨 🚩 🌡
☐ ☐ ☐ ☐ ☐ ☐ _____ _____

Firearm:	
Bullet:	Seating Depth:
Powder:	Grains:
Primer:	
Brass:	
Distance:	

Overall Results

☐ Poor ☐ Fair ☐ Good ☐ Excellent

Notes

_____
_____
_____

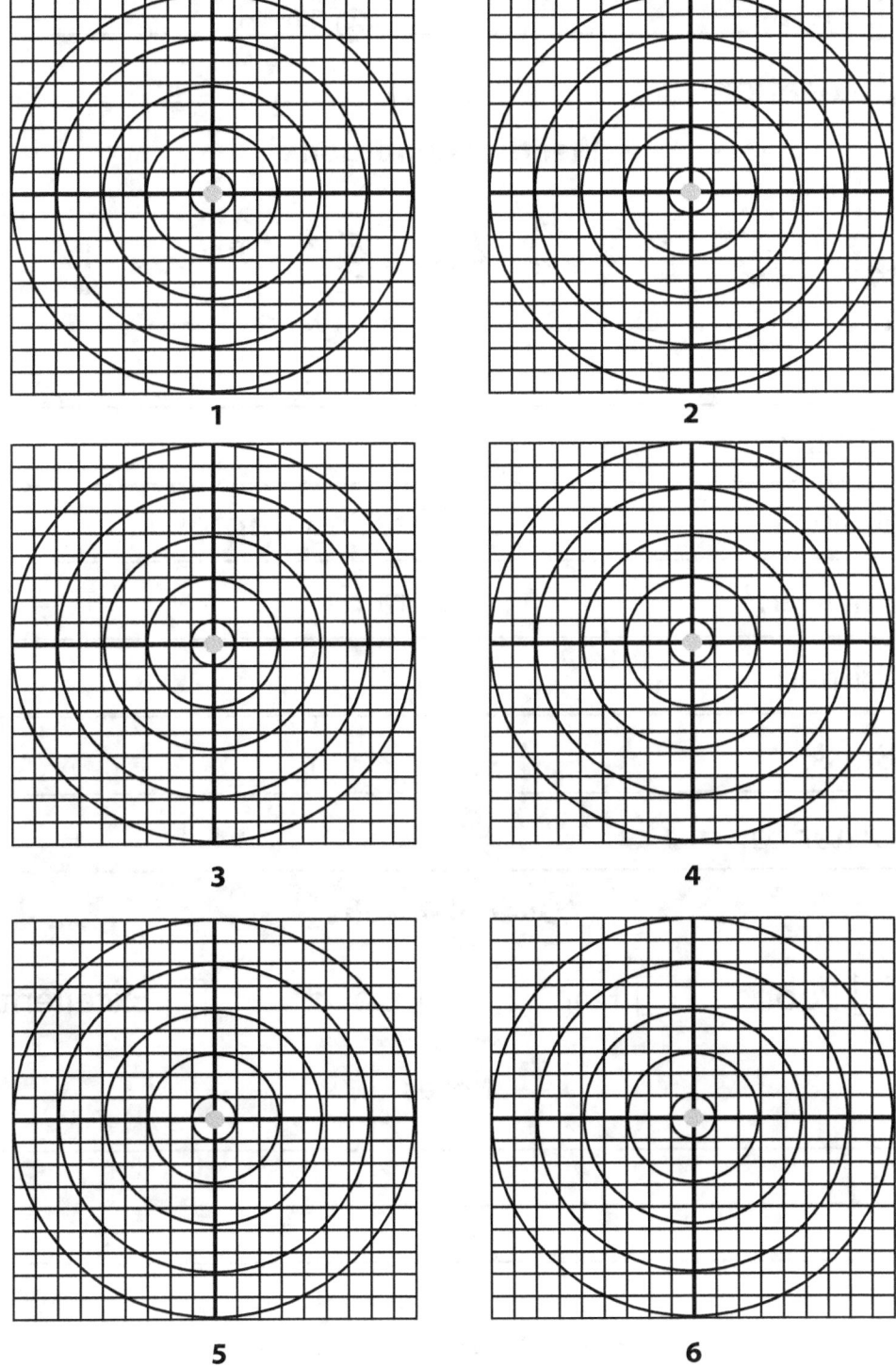

Date: _____ Time: _____

Location: _____

Weather Conditions

☀ ☐ ⛅ ☐ 🌤 ☐ 🌦 ☐ 🌧 ☐ 🌨 ☐ 🚩 _____ 🌡 _____

Firearm:	
Bullet:	Seating Depth:
Powder:	Grains:
Primer:	
Brass:	
Distance:	

Overall Results

☐ Poor   ☐ Fair   ☐ Good   ☐ Excellent

Notes

_____

_____

_____

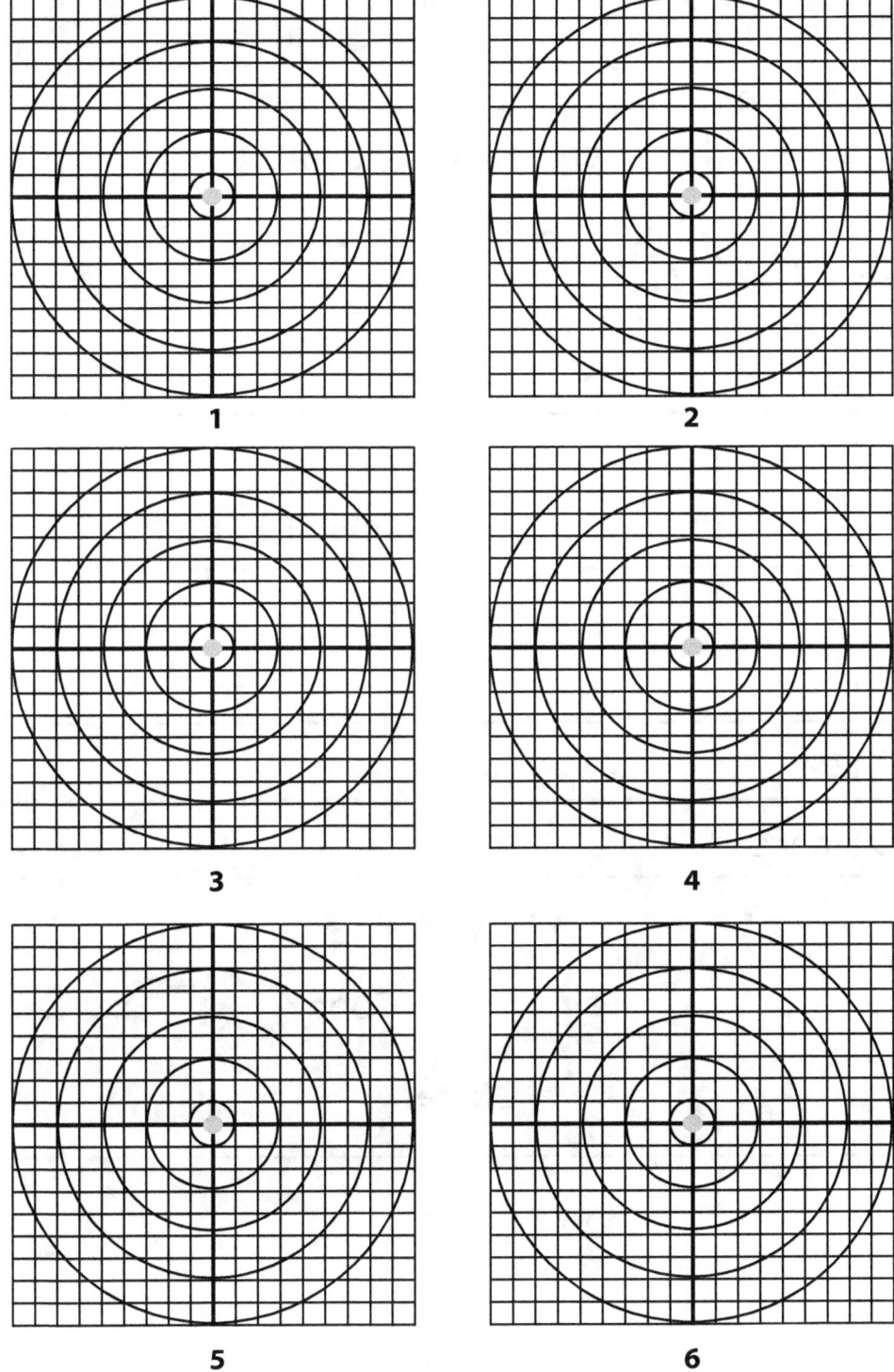

Date: _____ Time: _____

Location: _____

Weather Conditions

☀ ☁ ⛅ 🌦 🌧 🌨 🚩 🌡
☐ ☐ ☐ ☐ ☐ ☐

Firearm:	
Bullet:	Seating Depth:
Powder:	Grains:
Primer:	
Brass:	
Distance:	

Overall Results

☐ Poor   ☐ Fair   ☐ Good   ☐ Excellent

Notes

_____
_____
_____

☆ ☆ ☆ ☆ ☆

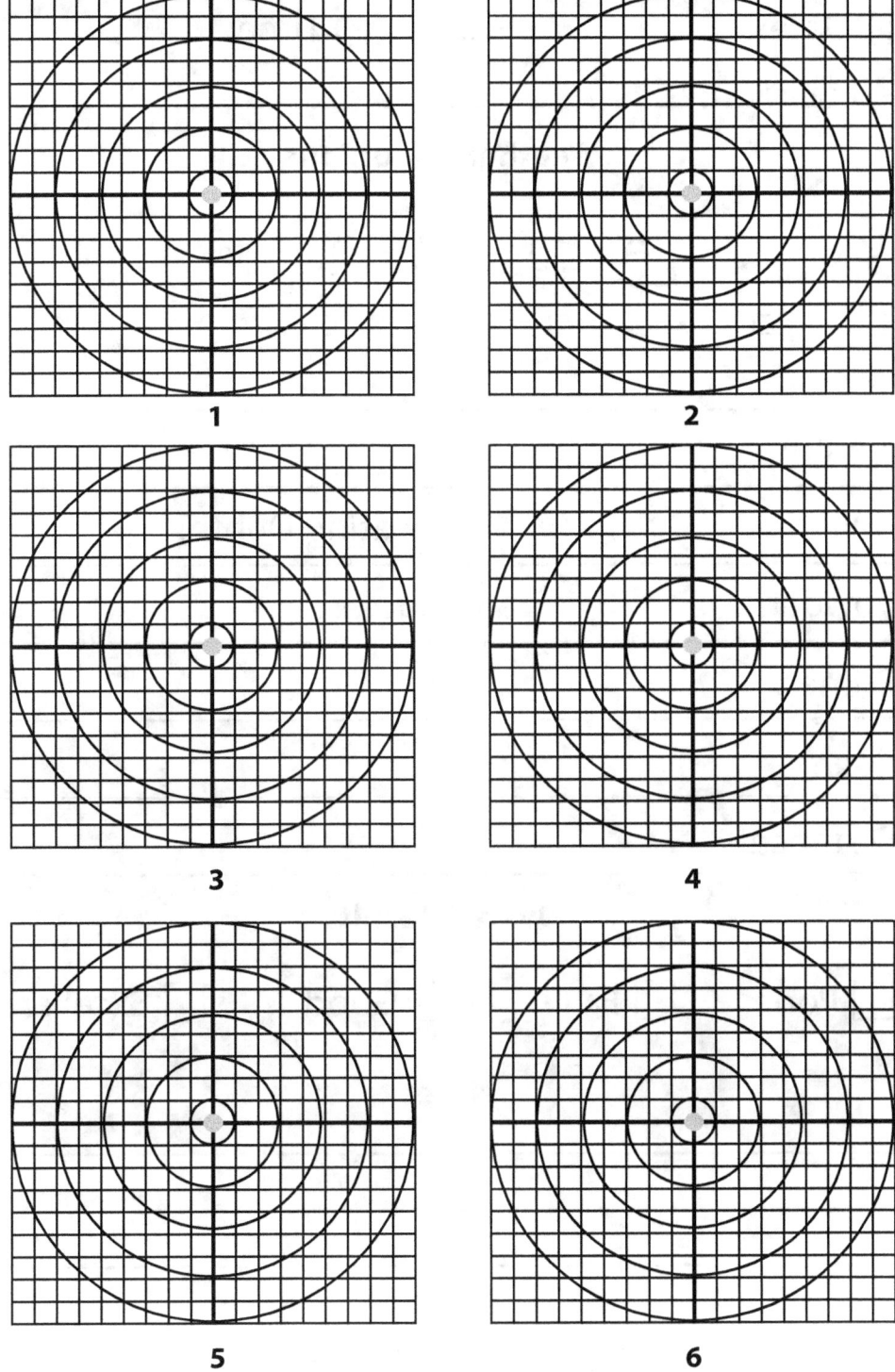

📅 Date: _____ 🕐 Time: _____

📍 Location: _____

Weather Conditions

☀️ ☐   ☁️ ☐   ⛅ ☐   🌧️ ☐   🌧️ ☐   🌨️ ☐   🚩 _____   🌡️

Firearm:	
Bullet:	Seating Depth:
Powder:	Grains:
Primer:	
Brass:	
Distance:	

Overall Results

☐ Poor   ☐ Fair   ☐ Good   ☐ Excellent

Notes

_____
_____
_____

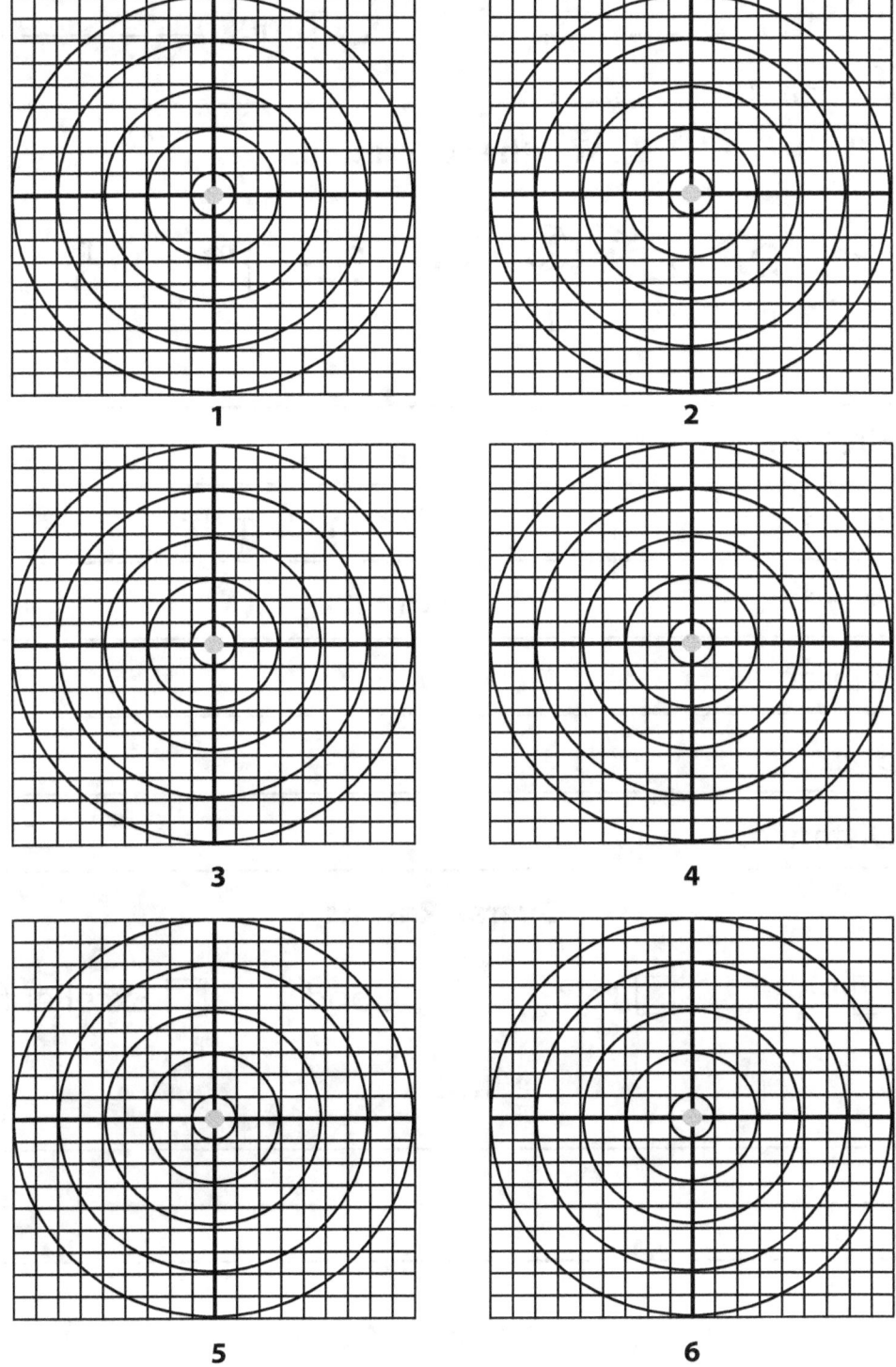

📅 Date: _____ 🕐 Time: _____

📍 Location: _____

Weather Conditions

☀️ ☐   ⛅ ☐   🌥️ ☐   🌦️ ☐   🌧️ ☐   🌨️ ☐   🚩 _____   🌡️ _____

Firearm:	
Bullet:	Seating Depth:
Powder:	Grains:
Primer:	
Brass:	
Distance:	

Overall Results

☐ Poor   ☐ Fair   ☐ Good   ☐ Excellent

Notes

_____
_____
_____

☆ ☆ ☆ ☆ ☆

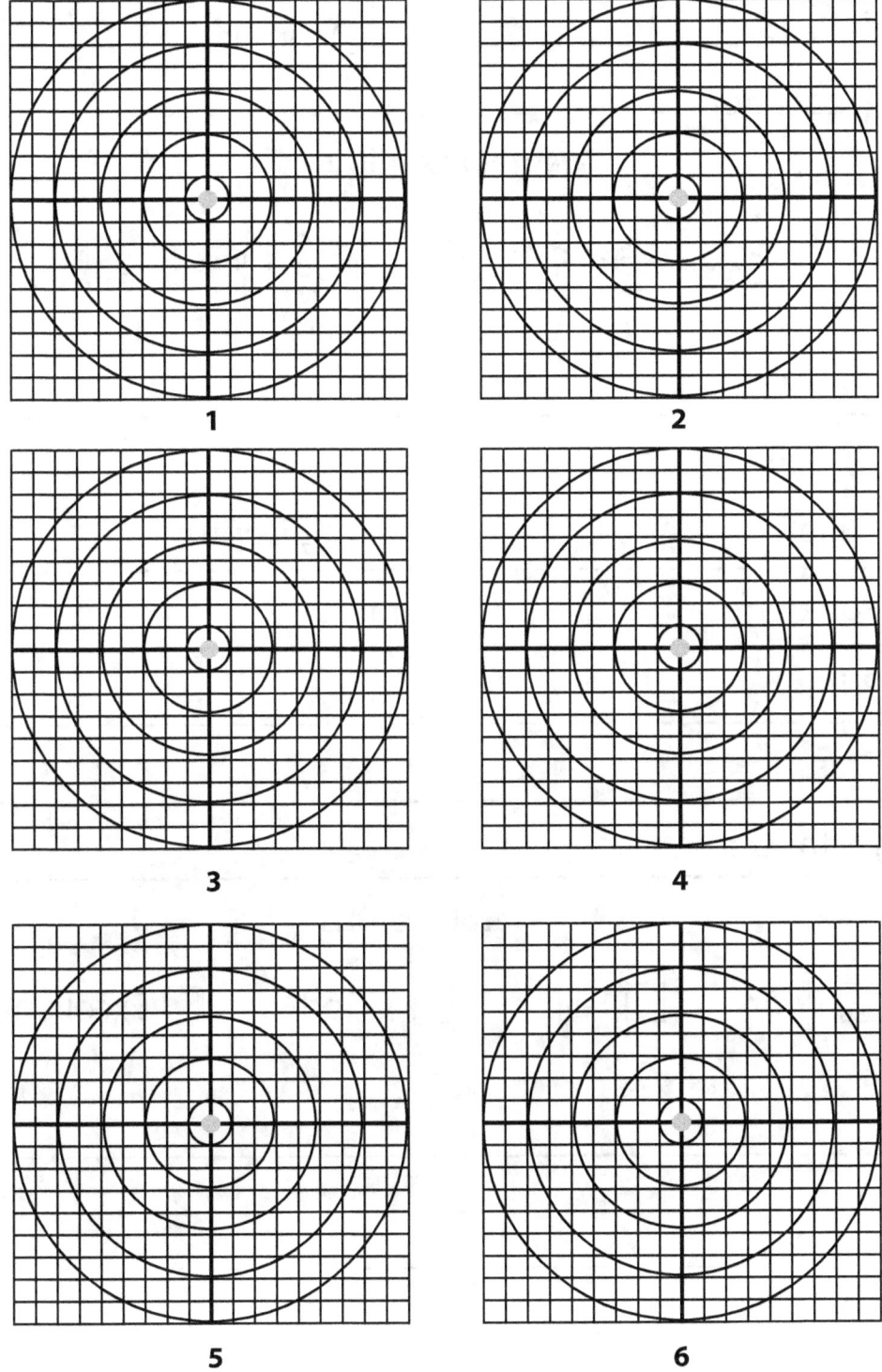

Date: _____ Time: _____

Location: _____

Weather Conditions

☀ ☁ ⛅ 🌦 🌧 🌨 🚩 🌡
☐ ☐ ☐ ☐ ☐ ☐ ____ ____

Firearm:	
Bullet:	Seating Depth:
Powder:	Grains:
Primer:	
Brass:	
Distance:	

Overall Results

☐ Poor   ☐ Fair   ☐ Good   ☐ Excellent

Notes

_____
_____
_____

☆ ☆ ☆ ☆ ☆

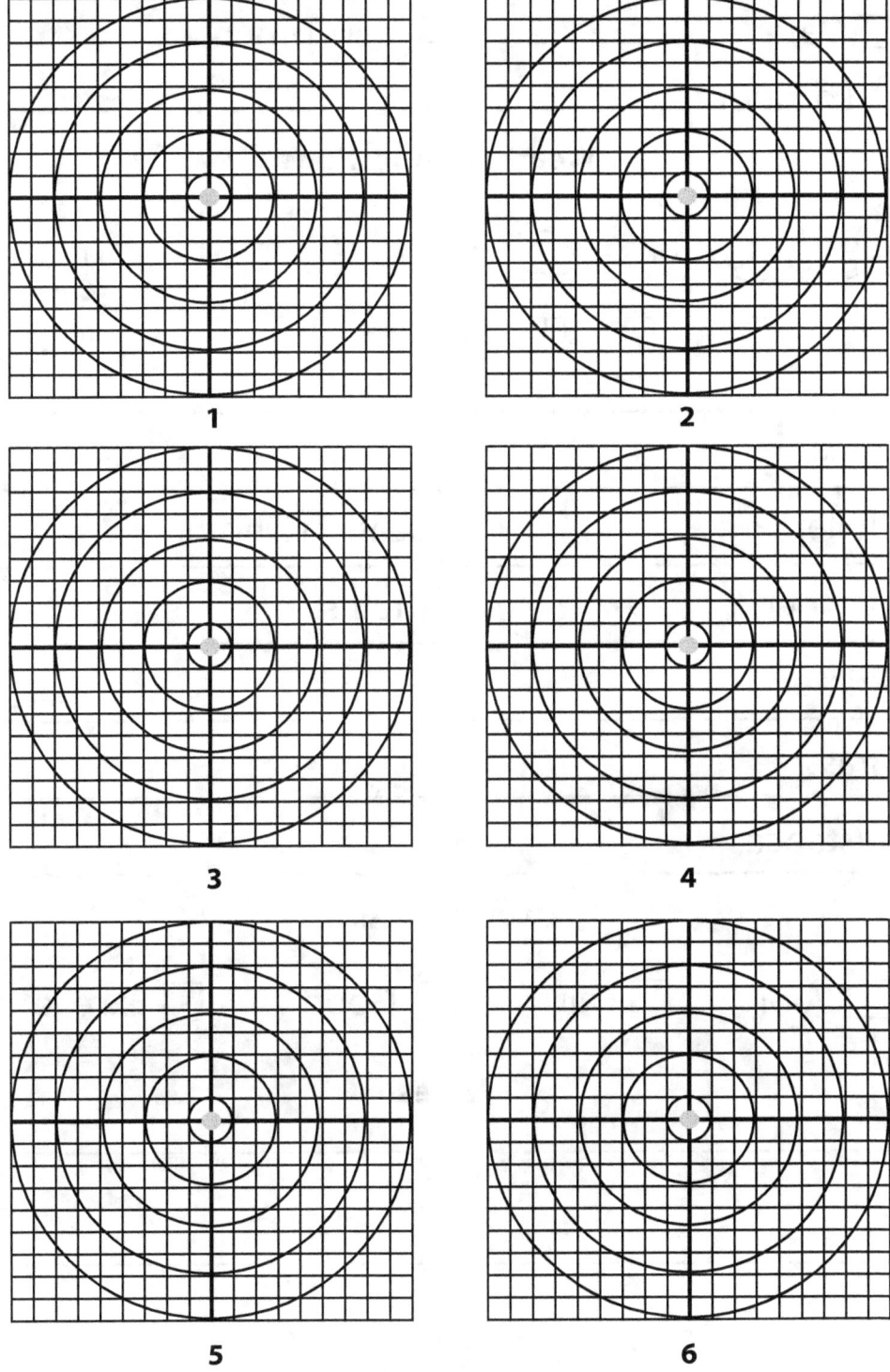

Date: _____ Time: _____

Location: _____

Weather Conditions

☀ ☁ 🌤 🌥 🌧 🌨 🚩 🌡
☐   ☐   ☐   ☐   ☐   ☐   _____   _____

Firearm:	
Bullet:	Seating Depth:
Powder:	Grains:
Primer:	
Brass:	
Distance:	

Overall Results

☐ Poor   ☐ Fair   ☐ Good   ☐ Excellent

Notes

_____
_____
_____

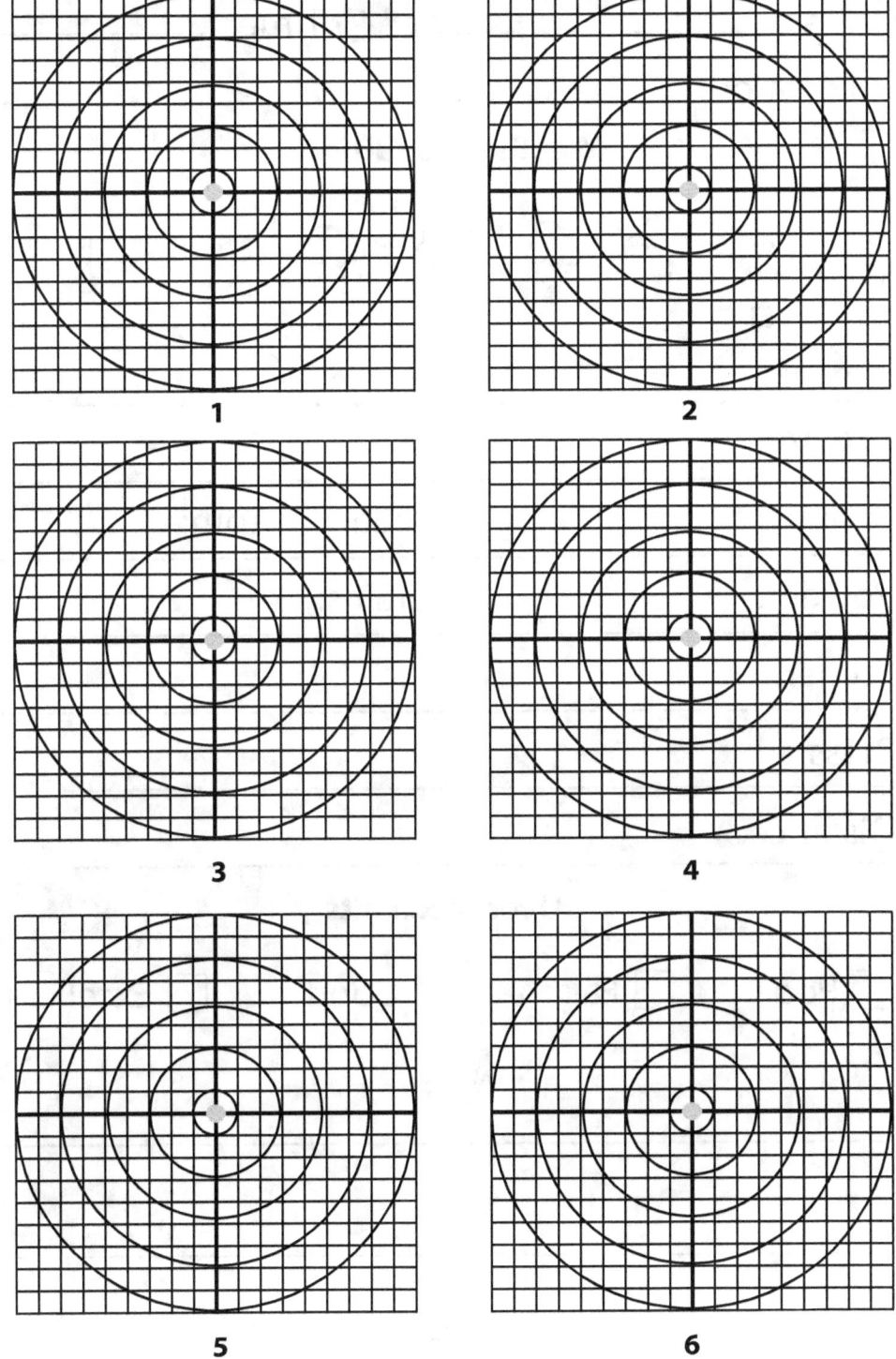

📅 Date: _____ 🕐 Time: _____

📍 Location: _____

Weather Conditions

☀ ☁ ⛅ 🌦 🌧 🌨 🚩 🌡
☐ ☐ ☐ ☐ ☐ ☐ ____ ____

Firearm:	
Bullet:	Seating Depth:
Powder:	Grains:
Primer:	
Brass:	
Distance:	

Overall Results

☐ Poor ☐ Fair ☐ Good ☐ Excellent

Notes

_____
_____
_____

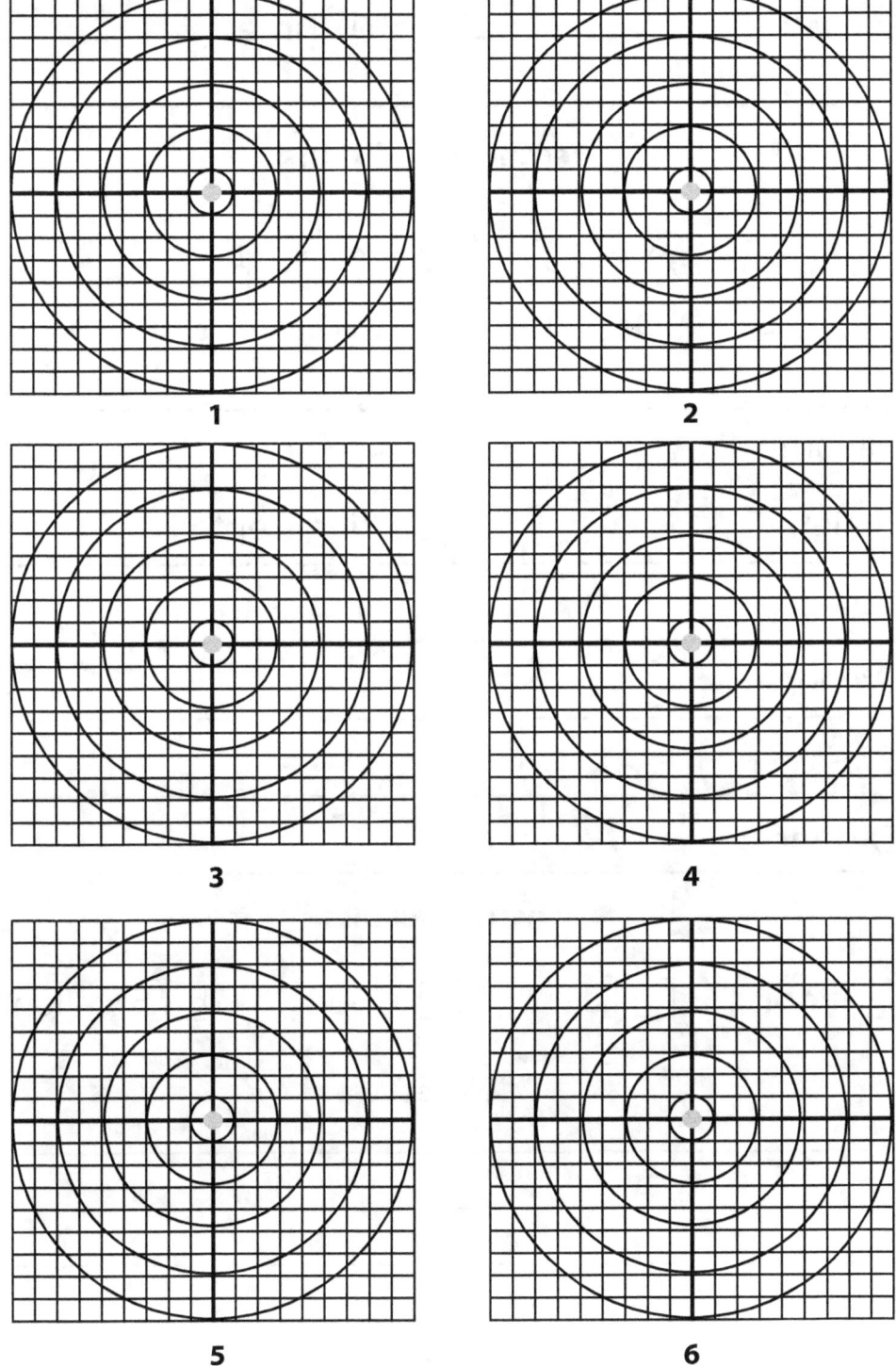

Date: _____ Time: _____
Location: _____

Weather Conditions

☀ ☁ ⛅ 🌦 ☁ 🌨 ⚑ 🌡
☐ ☐ ☐ ☐ ☐ ☐

Firearm:	
Bullet:	Seating Depth:
Powder:	Grains:
Primer:	
Brass:	
Distance:	

Overall Results

☐ Poor   ☐ Fair   ☐ Good   ☐ Excellent

Notes

_____
_____
_____

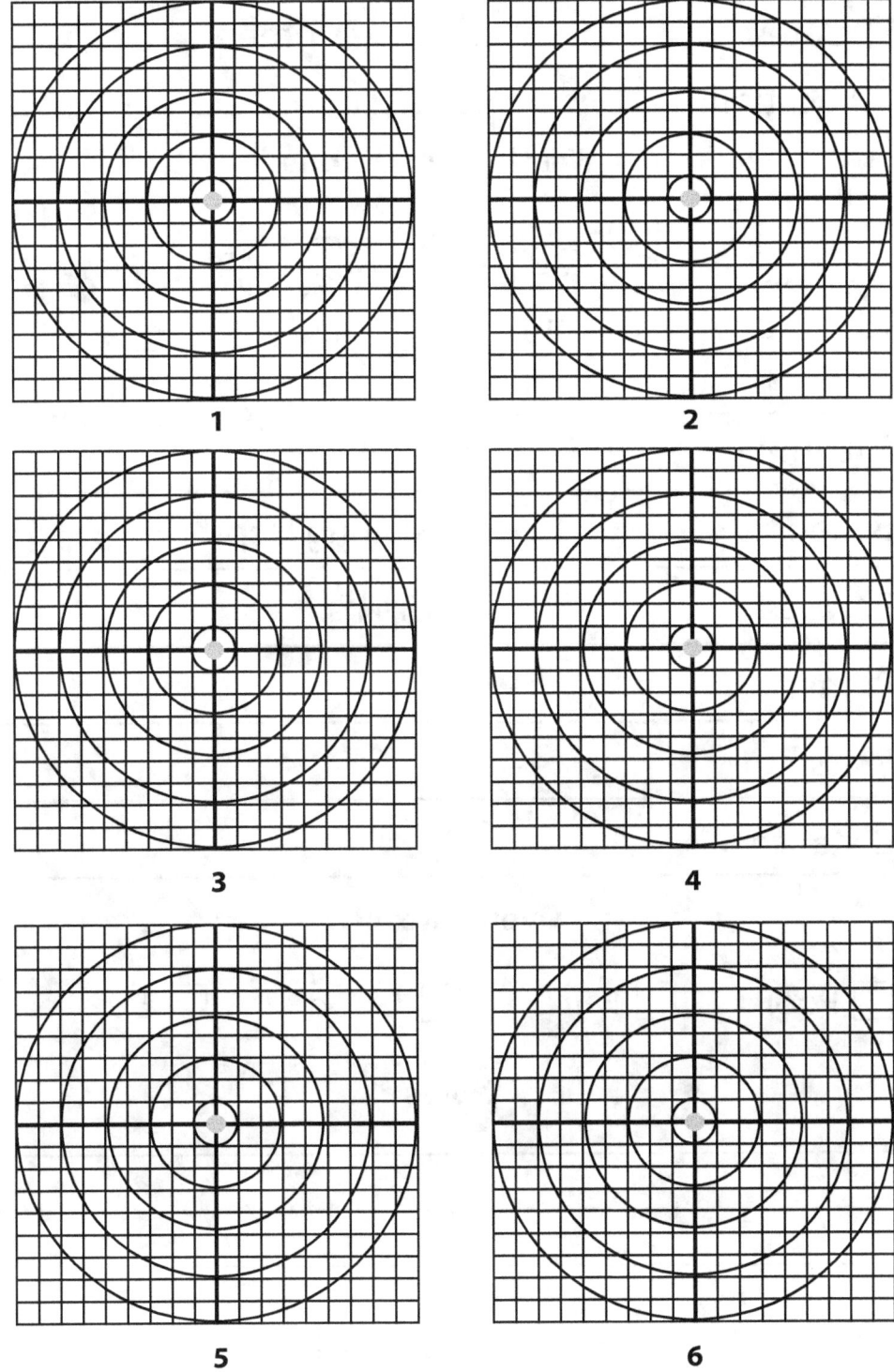

Date: _____ Time: _____
Location: _____

Weather Conditions

☀ ☁ ⛅ 🌧 🌧 🌨 🚩 🌡
☐ ☐ ☐ ☐ ☐ ☐

Firearm:	
Bullet:	Seating Depth:
Powder:	Grains:
Primer:	
Brass:	
Distance:	

Overall Results

☐ Poor   ☐ Fair   ☐ Good   ☐ Excellent

Notes

_____
_____
_____

www.ingramcontent.com/pod-product-compliance
Lightning Source LLC
Chambersburg PA
CBHW071125130526
44590CB00056B/2396